Balance

The Meno-Positive Chick's Guide to Creating a Balanced Life

DARLENE GAETZ
The Creator of Meno-Positive Chicks

Copyright © 2022 Balance by Darlene Gaetz
ISBN Number (Paperback) 979-8-88759-424-8
ISBN Number (eBook) 979-8-88759-425-5
www.meno-positive-chicks.com

All rights reserved. No part of this publication may be reproduced, distributed or transmitted in any form or by any means, including photocopying, recording or other electronic or mechanical methods without the prior written permission of the publisher, except in the case of brief quotations embodied in critical reviews and certain other non-commercial uses permitted by copyright law.

Although the author and publisher have made every effort to ensure that the information in this book was correct at press time, the author and publisher do not assume and hereby disclaim any liability to any party for any loss, damage or disruption caused by errors or omissions, whether such errors or omissions result from negligence, accident or any other cause.
Adherence to all applicable laws and regulations, including international, federal, state and local governing professional licensing, business practices, advertising and all other aspects of doing business in the US, Canada or any other jurisdiction is the sole responsibility of the reader and consumer.

Neither the author nor the publisher assumes any responsibility or liability whatsoever on behalf of the consumer or reader of this material. Any perceived slight of any individual or organization is purely unintentional.

The resources in this book are provided for informational purposes only and should not be used to replace the specialized training and professional judgment of a health care or mental health care professional.

Neither the author nor the publisher can be held responsible for the use of the information provided within this book. Please always consult a trained professional before making any decision regarding treatment of yourself or others.

For more information, email darlenegaetz@hotmail.com

Dedication

❋❋❋

To my husband, Rob,
for graciously enduring years of experimental dinners.

❋❋❋

To my kids, Ben and Rebecca,
for giving me unconditional love, support and gray hair.

❋❋❋

To my friends for sharing with me your guidance,
laughter and great coffee.

❋❋❋

To my stronger and wiser workout buddies
who keep me inspired with your zest for life.

Table of Contents

Dedication 3

Hello Friend 7

Introduction 9

Chapter 1: A Healthy Relationship with Food 13

Chapter 2: Sleep 21

Chapter 3: Finding the Calm Within 25

Chapter 4: Movement 31

Chapter 5: Community 35

Chapter 6: One Final Word 41

The Recipes 45

Breakfast & Brunch 47

    Country Brunch Pancakes 48

    Glazed Cranberry Scones 49

    Loaded Breakfast Oats 51

    Mamma G's Cinnamon Buns 52

    Overnight Chicken Dijon Strata 55

    Pumpkin Glory Muffins 57

    Sausage & Egg Stuffed Croissants 59

    Savory Cheese Scones 61

Soups, Salads & Sandwiches 63

    Arugula Salad with Creamy Champagne Dressing 64

    East Coast Seafood Chowder 65

    Kale & Bulgur Salad with Balsamic Vinaigrette 67

    Mamma G's Potato Salad 69

    Roasted Broccoli Sandwich 71

    Roasted Butternut Squash Soup 73

  Spinach & Feta Turkey Burgers 75

Comfort Foods 77

  Baked Mac & Cheese 78

  Basil Pesto Pizza 80

  BBQ Chicken Pizza with Creamy Ranch Dressing 82

  Beef Stroganoff 83

  Chicken Stew with Fluffy Dumplings 85

  Creamy Pesto Pasta with Turkey Meatballs .87

  French Acadian Rappie Pie 89

  Sheet Pan Lemon Chicken & Rosemary Potatoes 91

  The Best Potato Gratin 93

Sweet Treats 95

  Apple Crumble 96

  Apple & Stilton Crumble 98

  Canadian Butter Tarts 99

  Chocolate Cake with Marshmallow Frosting 101

  Layered Lemon Cheesecake 103

  Oatmeal Chocolate Chip Cookies 105

  Sourdough Bread Pudding with Sweet Rum Sauce 106

Odds & Sods 109

  3-Cheese Blend 110

  Balsamic Vinaigrette 111

  Breadcrumbs 112

  Breakfast Oats 113

  Buttermilk 114

  Cardamom & Banana Filling 115

  Chunky Cinnamon Applesauce 116

Creamy Champagne Dressing 117
Creamy Jalapeño Sauce 118
Creamy Ranch Dressing 119
Date Paste 120
Fresh Basil Pesto 121
Greek Tzatziki Sauce 122
Hollandaise Sauce 123
Homemade Pizza Dough 125
Icing Sugar 127
Lemon Curd 128
Lemon & Dill Dry Spice Mix 129
Lemon Zest & Lemon Juice 130
Oat Flour 131
Pickled Red Onions 132
Plump Raisins 133
Poultry Seasoning 134
Pumpkin Pie Spice Seasoning 135
Ranch Dressing Dry Spice Mix 136
Roasted Broccoli 137
Sausage Patties 138
Stabilized Whipped Cream 139
Sweet Rum Sauce 140
Toasted Nuts 141

Conclusion **143**
Acknowledgments **145**
About Me, the Author **147**

Hello Friend

In a way, this book has been a work in progress for the past twenty years. I always knew I wanted to create a recipe book, but deep in my gut I had a feeling it needed to be more than just recipes. I wanted it to have real substance like a carb-heavy meal, you know what I mean? Unfortunately, the added pressure of making it perfect and balanced made it difficult for me to move my feet on this project. With too many irons in the fire and pots bubbling over, this idea went nowhere for many years.

In 2013, my friend Jennifer and I discussed working on a different book together about menopausal women and how to find more balance in the next chapter of their lives. Now, I must tell you in case she is reading this that she hadn't yet reached that stage of her life, while I was right in the thick of it. It was interesting to view things through two different sets of lenses. We racked our brains to come up with a name for our new adventure, and one day, her husband said, "What about Meno-Positive Chicks?" Oh My Gosh, it was brilliant!

Yet, as excited as we were about this concept, Jennifer and I ended up doing absolutely nothing with our book idea. It was like that recipe you print out, meaning to try it but end up throwing away months later when you haven't done a darn thing with it. Jennifer went on to pursue other passions, and I decided to try different and easier ways to get these ideas out there, because in all honesty, the thought of publishing a book scared the pants off me.

Those other ideas worked…for a while until March 28, 2022. I was lying in bed and reflecting on how wonderful life was while saying a prayer of gratitude. But that day, something was different. On that day, my birth certificate said I had become sixty-one years young. Holy snickerdoodles! It seems like just yesterday I was forty (I really wanted to say thirty but felt like that would be pushing it a little bit).

On that particular morning, as I took in three big breaths and slowly let them out, I had a feeling it was time for me to take action with my book.

Some people receive messages from the universe that are soft and gentle, but not me. I get punchy, straight-to-the-point messages that usually leave me howling with laughter. This makes perfect sense for me since I've always believed laughter is good medicine for the soul. "Darlene, stop procrastinating," the universe told me. "If you don't do this right now, you never will. So, get off your tooshie and just do it!" The humorous presentation of this message certainly caught my attention, and I knew this was the day I would start putting pen to paper and writing this book.

But there was still a problem. While I had a ton of recipes, this project just didn't feel complete as a straightforward recipe book. That's when I realized the missing link was the material Jennifer and I had worked on years earlier to help menopausal women create balance in their lives. Once she gave me her blessing, there were no more excuses. It was time for me to get down to business.

So, here we are, and I must tell you I'm both excited and terrified at the same time, wondering whether you'll like this book or not. But if there's one thing I know for sure, it's that we cannot allow fear to keep us from doing something we are passionate about. Well, that and the fact that I am getting older and that little voice inside keeps reminding me, "You don't want to die with the song still within you, so move it, sister!"

Face the fear, my friend. Pursue your passions with confidence and no more procrastinating! Today is the day you could take that first step toward making your dream a reality. I'm happy I finally did, and who knows? It may even help you on your journey to creating balance.

Introduction

Balance is not something you find, it's something you create.
—Jana Kingsford

How Do We Create Balance?

Please tell me I'm not alone when I say the closer I get to my "expiry date," the longer I want to live. But not *just* live. I want those years to be epic quality years! I think we all want to be happy, healthy and have more balance. Just a sec…can we really have balance? I mean, sure, people are always talking about it, but do you see them really living it? Food for thought, but hey, what if we could truly live a more balanced life?

Something tells me we've been looking at this all wrong. It's the bigger picture, the holistic approach, that we should be looking at because if you think about it, everything works together synergistically, doesn't it? If a chair was cracked or broken on any part of it, the integrity of the entire chair would be in jeopardy. Call me crazy, but doesn't our life work the same way?

William Londen summed it up perfectly when he said, "To ensure good health: eat lightly, breathe deeply, live moderately, cultivate cheerfulness and maintain an interest in life." Seems simple enough, right? But how exactly do we do that? How do we find the right balance?

For starters, we don't find balance, we create it. We must take an active role in creating balance within our own lives. As I'm getting older and wiser, I've discovered five elements that, when working together, help us to create more balance.

To Create Balance, We Need To...

1. Have a healthy relationship with food
2. Get enough sleep and feel fully rested
3. Find the calm within us
4. Move our body more
5. Be part of a community

What You Can Expect in This Book

We often don't realize just how much hidden sugar, fat and sodium there is in processed foods. These additives make such foods highly craveable, immediately gratifying and easy to overconsume. However, they aren't doing our health any favors. In fact, they are causing us harm.

For this reason, I'm a huge fan of cooking from scratch as much as possible, and I truly believe it can help us find real balance in our lives. Wait, hear me out—cooking from scratch doesn't have to be difficult or time-consuming, yet there are a multitude of benefits. Preparing your meals at home saves money. Making your staple ingredients and spice mixtures in bulk saves time. Doing both can save your sanity, improve your health and enhance the quality of your relationships, all with a delicious home-cooked meal. For real, it's that simple.

I'm excited to share with you some of my favorite recipes that I have upgraded over the years to create healthier versions. Think less salt, less sugar and less fat. If you make a recipe and it tastes bland, don't get upset with the recipe. It simply means your taste buds are not used to less sodium or sugar in your food yet but give yourself a little time to adjust and you will soon find it tastes perfectly delicious and boosts your health.

What you won't find in this book are any calorie, fat, sugar, carb, protein or serving breakdowns, because you don't actually need to know those. Nutritional facts are important if you have specific health concerns, but they do nothing to help you create a healthy relationship with food. Because of this, you will also find recipes that I decided didn't need an upgrade. The most important thing is that you create

Introduction

balance between the two. Besides, some things just taste better with butter, sugar and cheese…just sayin.'

My wish is that you enjoy this book and all the recipes as much as I enjoyed putting it together. If I could offer just one piece of advice, it would be to keep an open mind and an open heart. It's never too late to bring more balance into your life and share it with others around you. If something brings you a little giggle, know that it's intentional. Laughter is good medicine for the soul, and don't we all need more of that in our lives?

Chapter 1

A HEALTHY RELATIONSHIP WITH FOOD

Healthy eating is a way of life, so it's important to establish routines that are simple, realistically, and ultimately livable.
—Horace

Cut the Negativity

Have you ever hidden in the kitchen to sneak just one more bite of cheesecake that ended up becoming an entire piece? Next thing you know, you feel guilty as all get-out and start beating yourself up over it, swearing you're going to hit the gym tomorrow and do extra time on the treadmill to make up for it. Or maybe you avoid certain foods all together, or even entire food groups, because someone on Instagram said they're bad. Does that mean you're bad on Friday night when you find yourself eating those foods? Maybe you wind up taking a laxative while beating yourself up for having no self-control.

Umm…do you hear those words? That is not a healthy relationship with food, fitness or yourself. The food isn't hurting you as badly as your negativity is. Sadly, I think we've all been here. Little by little, we've forgotten how to listen to and trust our own body to make healthy choices. Instead, we've allowed external sources to make all the decisions and tell us what our bodies need. We've allowed ourselves to use negative words to describe ourselves and food. We use food as a reward or punishment, and that's not okay.

This hasn't all happened overnight, but the good news is, we can take back control and change the narrative. Stay with me on this journey as I explain each aspect involved in gaining and maintaining a healthy relationship with your food, because it is possible, my friend.

Diets Suck

When you think of all the wasted years spent dieting with the latest trend or chasing after the next easy fix, don't you just shake your head in frustration? Where are the long-term, lasting results? Why do we feel the need to punish ourselves for gaining weight or reward ourselves when we lose some? Talk about a vicious cycle that is detrimental on our physical and mental health. We're going to drive ourselves insane with these yo-yo diets.

The reality is diets suck. No, really. Now that you're older, I hope you realize that diets were never intended to be a permanent solution to living a healthy, balanced lifestyle. The multi-billion-dollar dieting industry has trained us to see food in absolutes—they're either good or bad. That leads to us thinking of ourselves as good or bad for having those foods, but has that sort of thinking really ever benefited us? In this book, calling a food "good" or "bad" is going to be considered a curse word of the worst kind, so watch your mouth!

Emotional Ties to Food

Having a healthy relationship with food isn't just about the food we eat. It also involves our emotions that are lurking beneath the surface. It's important to understand how much food is attached to our emotions so we can gain control over it.

If you find that giving in to your cravings is becoming a regular pattern, then your lines are blurry and you need to readjust your focus. You're likely drinking or eating because of an emotional feeling such as boredom, frustration, anger, irritation or stress. But you have a choice: you can either be in control by recognizing the emotion and not reacting to it with food or drink, or you can give in to the instant gratification and then beat yourself up and allow the guilt, shame and negative self-talk to take control.

Ignoring our emotions is only a temporary fix, and it won't be long before the guilt, shame and negative self-talk starts up again. Where on earth does that awful cycle come from? Maybe it's a learned behavior, or maybe it stems from being on one too many restrictive diets over the years.

To borrow a line from *Forrest Gump*, "Life [is] like a box of chocolates. You never know what you're gonna get." We can't control what happens to us, but we can control how we respond. No matter what you're going through, it's important to recognize and feel all the positive and negative emotions and urges. The thing that we must fully grasp is our emotions won't hurt us. Allow them to be present without trying to fix them, cover them up or blame them on anyone else. Sure, it can be uncomfortable at first, but it will be far better for us in the long run.

Rewards & Punishments

Do you remember crying into a bowl of ice cream because of a breakup in high school? What about getting a treat as a child because you brought home a good report card or won your big game? How many glasses of wine or bags of Doritos did you have after that horrendous day at work? How did you feel afterward? Chances are that the answer is not any better than before you indulged.

I'm not a grandmother yet, but if I am ever fortunate enough to have grandkids, you can bet your Betsy bloomers I will not be rewarding or punishing them with food. Using food in this manner does not benefit us or create a healthy relationship with food, and it's time we changed the narrative for our kids and grandkids. Start setting a great example for them so when they're our age, they won't have to work as hard to train away their unhealthy relationships with food. Rather than using food as a reward and punishment system, we should be demonstrating how to find a peaceful balance.

Remove the Guilt & Shame

That's not to say you can never enjoy your favorite food or treat yourself to something special. While certain foods might not be providing your body with proper nutrition, sometimes you simply crave something "bad" for you (don't worry, I just popped a quarter in the cuss jar). It's perfectly okay to indulge on occasion. After all, life should be lived. So, enjoy the not-so-healthy-things from time to time, just do so in moderation and with *zero guilt attached*.

That's right—I'm telling you to not feel guilty when you do give in to your "guilty pleasures." It doesn't benefit you in any way to shame yourself; all it does is take away from your joy in that moment. If you can push aside the guilt and maintain a mindset of mindful moderation, you'll be able to appreciate your treats so much more.

Many self-proclaimed gurus will tell you to eat this, don't eat that. It's no wonder most people haven't a clue what it's like to have a healthy relationship with food. True, what we put into our bodies can have long-term effects, but it's about more than that. We need to learn to remove the guilt and shame because those don't do us any good either. You don't have to give up all your decadent treats and soothing comfort foods (in fact, I have recipes that fall under both of these categories in this book). You just need to create balance.

Two Simple Rules

Experts tell us to use food as fuel and nourishment for our bodies, and I couldn't agree more. We need to learn how to eat to live rather than live to eat. You should enjoy your food but having a healthy relationship with food means you feel in control around it, you don't look at it as either good or bad and, when you feel hungry, you eat only until comfortably full and don't stuff yourself. On the other hand, having an unhealthy relationship with food means that you're not able to recognize or manage your emotions attached to food, you lack awareness of your body's hunger and fullness cues and, if you're being honest, you don't really know what to eat to improve and maintain your optimal health.

So, what do you do to nurture a healthy relationship with food? Well, start by implementing these two rules into your life. Don't underestimate them—even though they look simple on paper, they might not be so easy for you to actually bring to fruition. But listen up, my friend: you've got this! As long as you're moving forward, you're not going backward. Every step is progress, so keep walking.

1. Rule 1: Clean Up Your Diet

A lifestyle of clean eating can help your body and brain function at its best, and if we really want to live a longer, healthier life, we need to start by cleaning up our diet. But what exactly is "clean eating?" Clean eating simply means choosing to eat more whole foods and less processed foods. This style of eating gives you the most nutritional bang for your buck.

Now, this doesn't mean you need to go empty your kitchen pantry of all those snacks and only have fresh veggies in the fridge. I'm also not telling you to avoid situations where you might be tempted. The truth is that no amount of preparation will stop you from living life or falling prey to temptation from time to time. There will always be parties, vacations, and busy times, but remember that you are in control, not your environment or situation. Learning to control our internal feelings is so powerful because it puts us in the driver's seat.

Still, there will be times in your life where things get turned upside down and you're going to feel as though there is no way you can manage your emotions, and that's okay. But when those seasons pass as they always do, remember what things you do have control over and what things you don't. Don't hide behind them or place blame. Recognize them and you will maintain the power.

What do you eat when you're trying to be clean? Well, it seems as if everyone has a different opinion on which way of eating is the best, but if you start by keeping it simple, you'll notice some immediate positive changes in your energy and stress levels. You might even find yourself sleeping better and feeling stronger emotionally. You see, every decision you make, when done consistently over time, has the potential to become a habit, and habits become a lifestyle, so choose wisely.

While everyone varies with their opinions on the exact details, here are some guidelines that most everyone can agree on.

Clean Eating

1. Limit processed foods, which generally contain higher levels of added sugar, salt and unhealthy fat.
2. Eat more whole grains and beans, which are loaded with fiber and other nutrients that help reduce inflammation and keep our gut healthier.

3. Eat more fruits and vegetables, which are naturally nutrient dense, make us feel fuller longer, help fight inflammation and keep the cells in our body healthy.

4. Limit alcohol, which can cause inflammation and contribute to other health issues.

5. Drink at least eight glasses of water every day to help your body flush out the toxins and boost your immune system. Fun fact: water is a natural headache remedy!

Rule 2: Practice Mindfulness and Moderation

Mindfulness is being present in the moment and really tuning in to your body. You become aware of what you're doing, the choices you're making and how you're feeling. In essence, mindfulness is you becoming an expert on *you*. No one can do that for you or better than you, so you really need to trust yourself here, my friend. This is not a "mess up once and I'm done" sort of thing either. Mindfulness takes patience, consistency and practice.

Maybe you went too long without eating, scarfed back a meal way too fast and then it hit you like a ton of bricks. Ug, being too full feels awful and all you want to do is sprawl out on the sofa. Not to mention when the negative self-talk gets going, before long, you're a horrible person who can't control yourself. Geez Louise! But hey, we've all done it. It's not the end of the world though. Use it as a lesson learned and grow from the experience.

Instead of repeating this cycle, start practicing mindful eating. Adding mindfulness to each meal gives your brain time to receive the signals that it's full, which leads to less overeating. Besides enjoying your food more, other added benefits to eating slower are that it makes you feel calmer, relaxed and more in control. It also helps your body absorb nutrients better, which boosts your health. Big bonus there, my friend!

Moderation is being aware of the middle ground between starving and stuffed. People who create a healthy relationship with food have built these skills through practice, which allows them to be mindful and tune in to their body's hunger signals.

The following are great questions you might want to ask yourself to navigate this middle ground between starving and stuffed.

Am I Really Hungry?

1. Why are you craving something right now? Are you bored, upset, lonely, stressed or tired? Take note of this and write it down.
2. How hungry are you? Use a scale of 1 to 10, with 10 being you would eat anything put in front of you right now, including your least favorite dish.
3. Are you actually hungry or just thirsty? Drink a glass of water and wait twenty minutes for the answer. Sometimes our brain mistakes thirst for hunger.
4. Are you satisfied? You *know* this feeling. Sure, you could eat more for taste, but you feel perfectly satisfied right now without that miserable bloated feeling.
5. Do you really want to finish this, or could you save it for later? Leftovers make for a great lunch the next day, by the way.

The skill of listening to your body and learning what works for you is just that, a skill, but with time and practice you can master it. Practicing both mindfulness and moderation means you will need to make some choices. But the more you understand your body and the food that makes you feel great, the easier it will become. Eating well will become an automatic healthy habit that keeps you feeling great and thriving in multiple areas of your life. Restrictive diets and cheat days have taken the thinking and choices away from us, which also takes away our power and accountability. It's time to take back your power, my friend!

HOT FLASH TIPS

1. *Add one extra serving of vegetables and fruits to your diet per day, don't skip meals and make sure you're drinking enough water throughout the day.*
2. *Eat at least one of your meals sitting down in a relaxed setting, even if you feel rushed. Eat slowly and mindfully.*

Chapter 2

SLEEP

Sleep is the golden chain that ties health and our bodies together.
—Thomas Dekker

Natural Circadian Rhythms

I'd like to think we learned something during the pandemic about slowing down, but we didn't. We live in a fast-paced society, where getting a proper rest is vital not only to our physical well-being but our mental well-being too. We need sleep because it helps to balance our hormones, affects our mood and energy levels, allows our body to repair and grow muscles and affects our memory and learning capabilities. When we don't get enough quality sleep it negatively affects our immune system, increases our stress hormones and can wreak havoc on our ability to make healthy, nutritional choices.

We all have a twenty-four-hour internal clock called the circadian rhythm that controls when we feel tired enough to sleep and when we're ready to be awake and face the day. It's natural to have most of your energy early on and become more tired throughout the day. Unless you're dead, that clock will continue to tick no matter what. Because of this, it's very important that we allow ourselves to get proper rest so we can power through our daily requirements.

Natural light plays a big part in our sleep pattern. I really noticed this when we lived in the Yukon Territory where, in the winter months, it doesn't get light until almost noon and starts getting dark by 4:30 p.m. In the summer months, it stayed relatively light all night long. Thank goodness for vitamin D, happy lamps and blackout curtains.

The way light normally works is when it starts getting dark, our body releases melatonin, a hormone that makes us feel sleepy. When it gets light, our body releases cortisol, a hormone that gives us energy. Given this information, you would think that most people in the Yukon Territory would be sleep deprived. Having lived there for thirteen years, I was able to function, but I didn't feel well most of the time. After doing some research, I learned that not getting enough sleep can lead to certain medical conditions, which could be why I felt healthier after moving to another province. Hmm...food for thought, or maybe something to sleep on?

Establishing a Routine

Ask anyone who knows me what time I go to bed and they will tell you, "Darlene is in bed by 9 p.m. and up at some ungodly time of the morning." The fact is, I sleep like a rock from 9 p.m. until 6 a.m.

I've developed some bedtime habits that work really well for me and I have been practicing them for years now. For example, when I get into bed, I go through a mental checklist to see if there is anything on my mind that I need to write down before drifting off. And yes, there have been times where I've hopped out of bed, written something down I didn't want to forget the next day and was able to drift off immediately once I got back into bed.

If you have difficulty falling or staying asleep, you might find you suffer from lack of willpower in other areas of your life. Have you ever found yourself missing fitness classes, ordering takeout, drinking way too much coffee and nipping at people or skipping a date with friends because you were too tired? Every choice you make is drawn from the same willpower tank, and lack of sleep will drain that bad boy right up!

You might be thinking, "So, what can I do about this?" I guess the obvious answer is get more sleep. I admit, sometimes that is easier said than done, so here are a few proven ways to help you get a better night's sleep. Please keep in mind there is no one-size-fits-all solution, so experiment with a few of these and find out what's right for you.

Chapter 2

Helpful Tips for Better Sleep

1. Stick to a sleep schedule, even on the weekends.

2. Unwind at least thirty minutes prior to falling asleep. That means no computer, TV, tablet or cell phone. Instead, use this time to quiet your mind. Practice yoga, relax in a warm bath, drink a cup of herbal tea, listen to a guided bedtime meditation or just lie there and allow your mind to settle down.

3. If your mind is racing, settle it by writing those thoughts in a notebook or journal. It's a great idea to keep a notebook and pen right by the bed.

4. If you wake during the night, don't check the time. As tempting as it can be, it can also make you anxious. Surprisingly, you might even develop a habit of waking up at that time every night, and you don't want that.

5. Pay attention to what and when you're eating and drinking. Are you doing so too close to bedtime? Are your foods or drink choices causing you to not sleep? Keep a food journal and see what patterns develop.

6. Move your body more during the day. People who get regular exercise sleep better because it increases serotonin and decreases cortisol. In essence, it's a natural sleep aid.

7. Make sure your pillows and mattress are fresh and clean. Your bed should be a virtual paradise to crawl into.

8. Declutter your bedroom so it's a place you look forward to relaxing in. This will also help you to quiet your mind.

9. Make sure your bedroom is quiet and dark. Give your brain all the help you can to shut down. Darkness triggers the release of melatonin, which will help you drift off.

10. Lower the temperature so it's cooler. It's difficult to sleep soundly when your body is overheating.

11. Check with your health provider and rule out a sleep disorder like sleep apnea.

12. Everyone is different, so listen to your body. See what works best to help you get the quality sleep you need and deserve.

HOT FLASH TIP

1. *Make sleep a priority just like you would any other activity. Don't make it the thing you do only after everything else is done. You need proper sleep in order to be efficient and productive during the day.*

Chapter 3

FINDING THE CALM WITHIN

Meditation is a vital way to purify and quiet the mind, thus rejuvenating the body.
—Deepak Chopra

Busy, Busy, Busy...

How on earth do we go about our day only to collapse into bed at the end of it, images of "things I have to do" filling our minds, and waking up even more tired than when we first went to bed? There is nothing calm or balanced about that, yet reality is we are a busy society with not much time left for living in the present moment.

We all love the quotes floating around social media about being present in the moment and living a balanced life. Some of us press that share button every time we see one! I must tell you though; I don't hear a whole lot of people actually living it. Many of us feel guilty for taking even a moment to ourselves, let alone an entire day, so how can we possibly be present in the moment when we're constantly thinking about the next one?

Instead, we distract ourselves and fill our schedules to the brim with unhealthy habits. In fact, it's almost frowned upon if you're *not* telling anyone who will listen how crazy busy you are! It's like a status symbol of our own importance.

But here's the thing, there's got to be a way to find some type of balance and happy medium in our lives. Otherwise, what's the point?

When we're constantly rushing about our day, we're going to get worn out quickly. It's time for us to practice what we preach and allow ourselves to take a breather, be present in the moment and enjoy life. Don't just dream about it, make it a reality.

Truly make rest and relaxation a regular part of your life. I promise, you will see a difference if you do.

Burnout Is Imminent

We all know the risk of going full-out too hard for too long. We're going to find ourselves in burnout land.

Some people actually joke about having a small health crisis just to get a few weeks off work. We all laugh and nod, knowing the feeling.

Wait just a second…do you hear yourself? What on earth are we thinking wishing for such a thing? Sure, some type of health crisis would force us to slow down and take a look at our lifestyle, but we shouldn't be waiting for a health crisis to assess our quality of life.

Start paying attention to what you're doing, how you spend your time and how you control (or don't control) your thoughts. Listen to your body and take care of it. If you need rest, take a rest. There is no reason to feel guilty for taking a moment to simply be present and enjoy life. In fact, your body needs those moments to recharge and refresh so you can operate at your best. Take care of yourself, my friend.

The Value of Meditation

In order to refresh, you will need to discover how to find the calm within. One of my favorite ways to do this is practice meditation. I know, I know. BIG topic here! Maybe you picture someone sitting in the lotus position, chanting, "Omm" Maybe you're thinking, "Holy mother of pearls, I'm going to burst if I try and fit one more thing into my day." Hang on though, it's not as scary as you might think, so take a breath and hear me out.

You don't really need to find any extra time for meditation. There are many ways to practice it, and yes, there are guided meditations, mantra chanting, vinyasa yoga and transcendentalism. But it can also be as simple as a breathing technique, being mindful of your present moment while walking the dog or saying a prayer. The bottom line is, it doesn't really matter which method or for how long you do it. What matters most is simply being able to quiet your mind and be present in the moment. A friend of mine put it this way: just shut the F up for five minutes.

Chapter 3

What Is the Right Meditation for You?

I learned how to meditate when I was fifteen. My parents decided our family needed to learn how to find the calm within, so we all went to a Saturday workshop that was held in an old farmhouse in the middle of nowhere. Normally when my brother and I were in situations like this, we could sneak away and return just before the *thing* was over, but this time, there was nowhere to sneak away to. So, we learned transcendental meditation and were each given a word or phrase to repeat to ourselves silently.

As it turns out, we both found it to be a life-changing eye-opener. My brother still practices transcendental meditation to this day. Me? Not so much. But I did discover I really enjoyed practicing mindfulness and movement forms of meditation. The point is, just find something that resonates with you, because the best form of meditation is the one you will stick with for the long-term, and therefore, gain the most benefits from.

Mindfulness & Movement

Mindfulness and movement are probably the types of meditation you hear about the most. The best part is you might already be practicing them without even knowing it. With both practices, the goal is to be aware of your thoughts as they come into your mind without focusing on them or placing any judgment. You simply notice them as if you are watching something cross the road in front of you, and then let it go as it disappears into the forest. This practice usually involves tuning in to your breathing. I love this part because controlling your breath can be done anywhere, anytime, with your eyes opened or closed.

> **Examples of Mindfulness & Movement Meditation**
> 1. Yoga is probably one of the most commonly thought-of forms of mindfulness and movement meditation. I don't consider myself a yogi, but I do enjoy it every once in a while. During yoga, you have no time to think about what you're having for dinner or that your shirt just slid up to your chin and revealed your tummy. You're too focused on bending and stretching your body as far as it can go while concentrating on your breathing. It can be difficult at

first and you may find yourself frustrated at your lack of flexibility or balance, but it does get better with practice, and before you know it, you'll be able to slide gracefully into a pose, close your eyes and just breathe.

2. Speaking of breathing, stop what you're doing right now. Step outside if you can or, at the very least, close your eyes. Take three to five deep breaths in, and then slowly let them go. This very short, but very powerful practice can help you reduce stress and make you feel more grounded.

3. Go for a walk while being aware of your body alignment, your steps or your breathing. I like to make up little affirmation songs and sing them to myself in the rhythm of my steps. For example, "I live a happy, healthy, balanced life and spread love and laughter wherever I go."

4. Prepare a meal in the kitchen. You need to eat anyway, so why not take this time to channel your inner chef or some long ago ancestor? Focus on the task at hand and don't rush through it. Enjoy the moment.

5. Have you ever walked barefoot in the grass or let dirt slip between the fingers of your bare hands? There's something powerful about connecting to Mother Earth. Get outside and into nature. With purpose, feel the connection to the earth and take deep breaths, allowing the energy around you to fill your soul. Take note of the swaying leaves in the trees, the birds chirping around you, and the breeze as it caresses your cheeks. What else do you hear, smell, or feel?

6. Listen to music. Depending on the mood you want to create, music can be good for the soul.

7. Do you play an instrument, sport, or have a favorite hobby? Focusing on something other than yourself means you need to be present in the moment and allow all the worries of the day to melt away.

CHAPTER 3

Practice Being Intentional

It's amazing what intentional meditation can do for you, not only spiritually but physically as well. Studies have shown that meditation lowers blood pressure, helps with depression and can even rewire the brain. It's true! Reports have shown that people are able to deal with stress and life a little easier when they add a meditation practice to their life. As the Dalai Lama once said, "Calm mind brings inner strength and self-confidence, so that's very important for good health."

The good news is that you don't have to meditate for hours on end to achieve such results. Simply start with five or ten minutes a day and work your way up to where you're most comfortable. If you don't have time for ten minutes, then you need to start with twenty…just sayin'.

I've also heard people say, "I tried meditation and I just can't do it." I'm calling B.S on that. Yeah, you heard me. Meditation is called a "practice" for a reason—it takes practice! True, meditation isn't all that easy. Yes, your mind will wander. But that's okay—simply notice it, let it pass and keep going. Over time, the frequency of your mind wandering will decrease. Be easy on yourself and remember, it's a practice.

HOT FLASH TIP

Choose one of the following to re-connect with yourself and find more calmness in your day today:

1. *As soon as your eyes open in the morning, while still lying in bed, take three slow, deep breaths in and out. Focus on being present in that very moment.*

2. *Get in the kitchen and make something that has a lovely memory attached to it.*

3. *Practice yoga. Yoga requires you to be present in the moment and breathe into the movement. Fun fact: people who practice yoga rarely fall into the habit of mindless eating, which makes them maintain their weight easier than others.*

4. *Go for a nature walk with no earbuds. Take in nature's music instead—the sounds and smells all around you can be truly beautiful and soothing.*

5. *Play your favorite music, move your body, and belt out the words. Music is good for the soul, increases your feel-good hormones and reduces stress.*

Chapter 4

MOVEMENT

We do not stop exercising because we grow old—we grow old because we stop exercising.
—Dr. Kenneth Cooper

Turn Back Time

Even if you haven't made exercise a regular part of your life, you must at least know that it's kind of a big deal. And no, it's not just about looking good—although come on, it's instinctive to want to look and feel our best, isn't it? Are you thinking of Cher right now singing "If I could turn back time" Ha! I thought so! But even more than that, scientists have discovered that regular exercise can turn back the hands of time. *Say what?* Let me repeat that: scientists are certain that when we make exercise part of our daily lives, our bodies actually change at the cellular level and our DNA starts to get younger. Let that sink in for a minute.

That's right, scientists have performed studies in which they researched the bodies of seventy-year-olds who made weight-bearing exercise part of their daily regime. They found that the stamina and muscular system of the seventy-year-olds were comparable to that of a forty-year-old. Holy moly, that blew my mind! I've also seen this in action. I work out at a gym with people of all ages, and I can tell you the older, wiser generation I work out with are incredibly fit! They're doing everything the younger people do. Yes, sometimes with slight modifications or with more recovery seconds in between, but they do it without whining or complaining. They're an inspiration to all those around them and it takes the scary right out of getting older.

I too am a living testament to this, my friends. I taught fitness on and off for many years starting in my twenties. Back then, we were told it was a normal fact of life that as we aged, our muscle mass would decline, and our bones would become fragile. Well, I'm here today at the age of sixty-one to say that I can still lift weights like I did in my twenties. In fact, my body feels stronger than ever. Of course, there are more wrinkles than there used to be, but there's not one fragile bone in this body.

The Fountain of Youth

There are so many physical and mental benefits to making fitness a part of our healthy, balanced lifestyle. Our muscle mass, bone density and strength increases. Our body fat and cholesterol levels decrease, and our immune system gets stronger, lowering our risk of getting heart disease and diabetes. Even our mood improves. I could go on and on, but I think you get the gist of it.

So, my friend, if you've been looking for ways to age gracefully and look younger, stop paying for expensive magic lotions and potions offering you hollow promises. The fountain of youth is literally inside you, and it's *free!*

Move Your Body

To access your own personal fountain of youth, you need to move your body. But what type of exercise should you be doing and how often? My quick answer is any kind of exercise you like, because that's what you'll be able to stick with on a daily basis.

Now, I don't mean to say you're locked into one exercise or routine every day forever after. You are allowed to change it up and have some easier or more enjoyable days. For example, I work out in the gym Monday through Friday with a combination of cardio and weight training. For me, this routine is nonnegotiable, and I look at it as if it's my job. I suppose in a way, it is my job to keep this body and brain in the best shape possible.

But the weekends? Those are purely for fun. On the weekends, I love to get outside for a nature hike, snowshoe on the mountain, take a walk around the neighborhood or simply putter in my garden. Getting outside makes me feel more grounded and energized. It lifts my spirits, boosts my self-esteem, allows me to relax and makes my life feel balanced. Bonus that it helps me move my body without even realizing it because I have so much enjoyment with the activity I am performing.

No matter if you're walking, gardening, hiking or simply collecting the mail, being outside means you're more active than you would be sitting inside surrounded by four walls. It puts you into an environment with more sights and possibilities. You can see something you wouldn't normally see, meet new people, and just feel good in general. The bottom line is when we feel we have a sense of control over our physical well-being, it gives us the emotional strength to make other positive changes in our lives.

And just like that, my friend, you are one step closer to living a happier, healthier and more balanced lifestyle.

HOT FLASH TIP

1. *Just like you schedule time for other important things in life, plan and schedule your exercise this week. Make it a nonnegotiable and see how you feel at the end of the week, after two weeks, after a month, and so on. I can almost guarantee that you will find a multitude of benefits, including feeling younger!*

Chapter 5

COMMUNITY

Our lives aren't just about us—they are also about our connections to other people.
— Laura Lynne Jackson

Connection & Laughter

No one really talks about this piece of the puzzle called community, which I find incredible. To me, it's right up there with your diet, exercise, sleep and calming the stress in your life. We're social creatures who are not meant to be alone, and it's important for us to foster and maintain healthy connections with family, friends, co-workers, neighbors and even acquaintances. Feeling connected to others allows us to be a part of something far greater than ourselves.

It doesn't matter where you are in life, we all need the physical and emotional benefits that come with being part of a community. Healthy relationships help to strengthen our immune system, increase our self-esteem and empathy for others, reduce our stress and anxiety levels and help us live longer, happier lives. Get outside and socialize. Crack some jokes and a smile. Share a warm embrace. Trust me, it will give you a boost.

Cut Out the Toxicity

Speaking of friends and family, let's get this out of the way right now. Do you have people in your life who are toxic? You know who they are, don't you? Maybe it's a family member always asking something of you even though they don't reciprocate the effort, but you feel guilty or obligated because they're family. Or the friend who never seems happy for you, mocks you for trying something new and makes you feel *meh* whenever you're around them.

Maybe it's time to set some healthy boundaries. I've been there myself a time or two, and oh my gosh, when you find your voice and set your boundaries, you will experience power and strength like you've never experienced before. That doesn't mean they're going to respect your boundaries, but you also don't have to allow toxic people to be in your life, whether they are family or friends. If you set your boundaries and they aren't respecting them, it's time to consider whether they bring enough value to your life to outweigh the toxicity. Chances are, they don't.

It can be difficult to cut people out of your life, toxic though they may be. You might find it difficult or cold-hearted or feel judged. But trust me when I say that when you get rid of the dead weight of those who only hold you back or bring you down, the doors will open up to allow other wonderful people in. There really are people out there who will respect your boundaries and make you feel strong, supported and appreciated. Go find them and surround yourself with the right people.

If we don't put healthy relationships near the top of our list, we're going to find our well-being near the bottom. The people you surround yourself with really do have a huge impact on your well-being, so do what you need to do in order to be well. Those who truly care for you will respect that, and those who don't, well, are they really bringing any value to your life or are they merely causing you harm?

Finding Your Tribe

Finding your tribe—those who want to see you succeed and be happy—is incredibly important. Since fitness has been a big part of my life for so long, one of my tribes is a group of fitness folks who all share a passion for creating and maintaining healthy bodies. We support and encourage one other as we're building muscle and perfecting our burpees, but we also laugh together—a lot. You need to find a tribe like this that can make you feel supported, connected and loved.

If you're not sure where to find your tribe, here's a few ideas to get you started.

Find Your Tribe

1. Is there a physical activity you particularly enjoy? Look online, in a local newspaper or at your fitness center to see where those things are being offered and join in the groups.

2. Do you enjoy volunteering? Look for organizations that support your values and join in.

3. Sign up for a class at your local community college or offered by your city and learn something new like playing an instrument, painting, pottery or studying a new language. The possibilities are endless.

4. Do you have a hobby such as quilting, birdwatching, fishing, reading or writing, a particular sport or collecting something? Look for others who share your interest. Join classes or groups who get together to do it and discuss it.

5. Are you really good at something specific? Offer to teach a class or lead a group discussion on it.

Laughter Really Is the Best Medicine

I meditate daily and, quite often, I'll see, feel or hear something funny, and you know what? That's the way I receive messages. It makes me look at the lighter side for answers. It's as if the universe knows I love to laugh, and even if I have something heavy on my heart, that little giggle gives me the strength and even the courage I need to feel more in control in an out-of-control situation. There really isn't anything quite like the power of a good laugh to bring you back into physical and mental balance.

Speaking of laughter, don't you find that laughing together creates a connection with people whether you know each other or not? If someone is going through a rough patch in life, giving them a smile or laughing over something silly can go a long way to helping them feel better, and even lift your spirits as well. When you're in line at the store and find some common ground to laugh about with the person behind you, it opens up the door to another connection, even if just for a moment. Those connections, whether fleeting or long-term, make us feel rooted in our community. It helps us to feel validated, important, and purposeful.

Laughter is good medicine for the soul my friend. It cultivates optimism, keeps us grounded, lightens our load and inspires hope, but did you know it's also good for our physical well-being? Yep, it floods our body with feel-good healing hormones that help reduce stress and anxiety, strengthens our immune system so we're better protected against illness, and it can help relax our muscles.

Laughter is contagious and it is another fun, powerful tool we all have access to for free. What's even better, the more you use, the more you create. So don't be stingy with your laughter. Share it with the world and watch it grow!

You Can Learn to Laugh Again

As I'm writing this, my heart feels a little heavy because I know not everyone laughs as easily as I do. We all come into this world as babies who naturally smile and giggle freely, but somewhere along the way, some of us seem to lose our sense of ha-ha. If you fall under this category, the good news is that you can learn to laugh again and, honestly, my friend, who couldn't use more laughter? Follow these tips—you can take them one at a time if that makes it feel less overwhelming—and you too will learn to laugh again.

Tips to Retrain Your Sense of Humor

1. Make a conscious effort to smile at people and notice how it makes you feel when they smile back.

2. Start reading funny cards in a card shop or bookstore. It's okay to giggle out loud. You might even have people come closer to see what you found so funny. Who knows? Maybe they need a good laugh in their day too.

3. Do you have grandchildren or pets? Play with them and laugh at the silliness that is bound to occur.

4. Laugh at yourself. Did you put hair cream on your toothbrush instead of toothpaste? This actually happened to a friend of mine when she was in a hurry one morning. Instead of getting frustrated, she laughed out loud at her mistake. Both tubes looked

similar, and I guess the universe was trying to tell her to slow down and be more mindful.

5. If you have access to social media, look for funny videos or memes and actively practice laughing out loud.

6. Put things that make you smile around your home. I have a painted turtle in my bathroom that my son made when he was little, and it always brings a smile to my face.

7. Make connections with people who enjoy life and look at the lighter side of things. I'm learning to play the ukulele, so I'm currently looking for a group where they don't take themselves too seriously, but rather just want to play and have fun.

HOT FLASH TIP

1. *Schedule time every day to actively look for something that makes you smile or laugh.*

Chapter 6

ONE FINAL WORD

We are what we repeatedly do. Excellence, then, is not an act, but a habit.
-Aristotle

Listen to Yourself

Our bodies give us signs all the time. More often than not, we don't listen. When we don't follow that intuition to do something for ourselves—something we know we need—that's when things can go downhill fast. Whether it's a physical health crisis, exhaustion, or feeling mentally overwhelmed, our bodies will get the message through to us somehow. So, listen up my friend because it's much better to hear the message sooner than later.

Finding Guilt-Free Balance

Finding a way to bring more balance into your life is not selfish. In fact, I will argue the opposite. When you feel balanced, you feel energized and inspired—you're more present in what you're doing each moment, more available to others and, dare I say, less apt to be short tempered, easily irritated and snappy…just sayin'.

But balance isn't all sunshine and roses, or kale and ground turkey. For some people, cleaning the dust and cobwebs out of their house or preparing meals for the week makes them feel on top of the world. For others, it can mean scarfing back a bag of Doritos all by yourself while binging Netflix. Who cares if it's not expanding your mind or connecting you to your spirituality?

No one ever said you had to be productive every second of every day. In fact, balance is quite the opposite. Balance is about taking the good with the bad, the healthy eats with the indulgent splurges, the intense workout session with the chill days. If you need a glass of wine or a slice of cake every so often, go for it. Just make sure to do so in moderation and don't attach any guilt to it. Allow yourself a moment of mindfulness and fully enjoy it.

Give Yourself Grace

As you're creating more balance in your life, don't be too hard on yourself. Reality check here: every single day is not going to be in balance. There will be some days, no matter how hard you try, that just aren't going to go your way. Trying to force each day to be balanced might even make you feel more out of balance because you're putting unfair stress on yourself to keep yourself in balance. Crazy, right?

Allow yourself some grace. Give yourself a day off (or an off day). Recognize the little victories. Just in case you need to hear this again, don't underestimate the small stuff. The little wins you have every day—choosing to take the stairs instead of the elevator, going for a walk instead of watching TV, doing a five-minute meditation instead of responding hastily to an ill-received text message or email, or opting for a smaller piece of that decadent dessert—all add up to a larger victory. Over time, these smaller habits become healthy habits that can change your life and even the lives of those around you.

Balance through Food

Food isn't just fuel for our body. It's also one of the ways we can show love to ourselves, our family and our friends. There's a reason families traditionally enjoyed their meals together. Gathering around the kitchen table should be a safe place where relationships are nourished and supported. In today's busy world, let's strive keep this tradition alive because our world needs it more now than ever.

As our population continues to grow, so do obesity, diabetes and heart disease. I know deep within my core that we need to take back control over what we consume. Healthy eating is vital to our well-being and survival. If we are always eating on the go, we will make poor choices. On the other hand, if we start reintroducing the concept of sharing meals, we will slow down and be more mindful. Occasional indulgence is okay, and even welcomed, but it must be done with mindfulness and in moderation.

Cheers to creating balance, my friend!

HOT FLASH TIP

1. *Fun fact, people who allow themselves to enjoy what they eat in moderation without paying attention to the nutritional labels tend to eat more nutritiously and maintain a healthy weight. So, go ahead and enjoy a few of the following recipes with zero guilt, eat mindfully and show your body the love it deserves.*

The Recipes

And now, the recipes that can help you
on your journey to create balance!

HOT FLASH TIP

*Whenever you see an * next to an ingredient in a recipe, it means you can find a recipe for that ingredient in another location of this cookbook.*

Breakfast & Brunch

One cannot think well, love well, sleep well, if one has not dined well.
—Virginia Woolf

COUNTRY BRUNCH PANCAKES

Move over flat, floppy pancakes and make room for these bad boys! My mother made these a lot when I was a teenager, but since then, I've tweaked the recipe to where it is today. They're bigger, denser, and very filling. They're a little crispy around the edges with a lovely soft texture inside. Serve with maple syrup, sliced fruit or my Chunky Cinnamon Applesauce*. You can also use this same recipe for waffles.

INGREDIENTS

1 cup low fat cottage cheese

1 cup low fat plain Greek yogurt

1 cup boxed egg whites

1 TB brown sugar

Lemon Zest* from 1 lemon

1 1/4 cup all-purpose flour

1 1/2 tsp baking powder

DIRECTIONS

1. In a bowl, combine the cottage cheese, yogurt, egg whites, brown sugar, and lemon zest.
2. In a separate bowl, sift the flour and baking powder together, and then stir the flour mixture into the liquids.
3. Using 1/3 to 1/2 C of the batter, cook over a low to medium heat in a well-greased pan or on a griddle until golden brown on both sides.

HOT FLASH TIPS

1. Add a little more butter to the pan after each batch and make sure to not crowd the pan for easier flipping.
2. Because the batter is thick, you'll be tempted to flatten them, but don't. Just spread them out a little bit.
3. These freeze really well if you want to make a large batch or have leftovers.
4. Save the egg yolks and use them to make something else, such as Hollandaise Sauce*.

GLAZED CRANBERRY SCONES

As an east coast Canadian, scones are part of my DNA. This recipe has had a few overhauls over the years, but I think you'll enjoy this version with its zippy little cranberry bits and sweet lemony drizzle. Great for brunch with a fruit and yogurt parfait or for a little afternoon snack with a big cup of coffee or tea.

INGREDIENTS

2 cups all-purpose flour

$1/3$ cup sugar

1 TB baking powder

$1/4$ tsp sea salt

2 tsp Lemon Zest*

$1/3$ cup frozen butter, grated

$1/2$ cup cranberries, chopped

$1/2$ cup pecans, chopped

1 cup plain Greek yogurt

Glaze

$1/2$ cup Icing Sugar*

2 tsp freshly squeezed Lemon Juice*

DIRECTIONS

1. Preheat the oven to 425°F.
2. Whisk the flour, sugar, baking powder, salt and lemon zest together.
3. Crumble in the butter until it resembles coarse crumbs. Add in the cranberries and pecans. Gently stir in the yogurt until it's just moistened.
4. Turn out onto a floured surface and shape the dough into an 8- to 10-inch circle. With a sharp knife, cut it into 4, 6 or 8 wedges.
5. Place the wedges on a baking pan lined with parchment paper, making sure they don't touch so that all the sides can get crispy.

6. Bake for 12 to 14 minutes or until they're golden. Remember, every oven is different so watch the time.

7. Whisk the glaze ingredients together and set it aside.

8. Remove the scones from the oven and place them on a cooling rack for 10 minutes to cool down before you drizzle on the glaze.

HOT FLASH TIPS

1. *Try replacing the cranberries with blueberries, blackberries, or raspberries—any of these would also pair beautifully with a lemon glaze.*
2. *Icing Sugar* can be substituted with powdered sugar, but granulated sugar is not the same. If all you have is granulated sugar, you could make your own Icing Sugar* with my simple recipe.*

LOADED BREAKFAST OATS

Don't underestimate the power of oats, my friend. I eat this in a big bowl every morning before going to the gym. Oats are a complex carb, easy on the tummy and will give you loads of energy, especially if you use it as a pre-workout meal like I do. These are super easy to make, absolutely delicious and such an easy way to sneak more fruits and veggies into your day. Veggies? Say what?

INGREDIENTS

- 3/4 cup water
- 1/2 cup milk
- 1/2 cup quick cooking steel cut oats
- 1/2 cup riced cauliflower
- 1/2 tsp cinnamon
- 1 TB ground flaxseed or hemp hearts
- 1/4 cup unsweetened apple sauce
- 1 medium banana, sliced
- 1/2 cup blueberries
- 1 tsp maple syrup or honey to taste

DIRECTIONS

1. In a medium saucepan, mix the water, milk, oats and cauliflower rice together. Cook over medium heat for about 5 minutes or until the oats have softened and the mixture has thickened.
2. Turn the heat off and stir in the cinnamon, ground flaxseed or hemp hearts and applesauce.
3. Pour it into a bowl, top with banana slices, blueberries and a touch of maple syrup or honey.

HOT FLASH TIP

1. Have an Instant Pot? Make a large batch of Breakfast Oats* to keep in the fridge for quick breakfasts during the week!
2. Both flaxseed and hemp hearts are high in calcium, fiber, potassium, protein, Omega 3 and Omega 6 fatty acids. Talk about a lot of power packed into a little seed!
3. You can substitute Date Paste* for the honey if you want to give this recipe a healthy boost.

MAMMA G'S CINNAMON BUNS

You're going to love these soft, rich, gooey cinnamon buns that my family has been enjoying annually for the past thirty years. Every Christmas morning, the kids would wake up to the smell of fresh cinnamon buns warm from the oven, and they still get all pouty if I talk about skipping them one year. In all honesty, they're pretty easy to put together, especially if you use a bread machine or stand mixer, but you can also make these by hand and enjoy the process. When I go this route, I feel connected to the women from generations ago and how proud they must be that I haven't forgotten them.

Preparing these the day before means a more relaxed morning with your loved ones. The caramel sauce comes from my husband's mom who always made them this way, while the cream cheese icing is what I was always more familiar with. Yes, these are absolutely sugar overload, which is why we only have them once a year. These buns rise up to be big and beautiful, so I bake them in my old rectangular Corning Ware pan that measures about 10x15. If you don't have one of those, use two 9x13 pans.

INGREDIENTS

Cinnamon Bun Dough

1 cup warm water	1 tsp sea salt
1/4 cup warm milk	$1/3$ cup butter, softened
2 eggs	4-5 cup all-purpose flour
$1/4$ cup sugar	2 1/4 tsp instant dry yeast
$1/4$ tsp ground nutmeg	

Cinnamon Filling

$1/4$ cup butter, softened	$1/3$ cup brown sugar
$1/4$ cup unsweetened applesauce	1 TB cinnamon

Caramel Sauce

1 cup cream
1 cup brown sugar
$1/2$ tsp cinnamon

Cream Cheese Icing

4 oz full fat cream cheese, softened	1 tsp freshly squeezed Lemon Juice*
2 TB butter, softened	1 cup Icing Sugar*

DIRECTIONS

Cinnamon Bun Dough

Place all ingredients into the bread machine in the order listed, starting with the milk and ending with the yeast. Set the machine to the dough cycle. Start with 4 cups of flour and add more if needed.

Cinnamon Filling

Mix the butter, applesauce, brown sugar and cinnamon together. Set aside until needed.

Caramel Sauce

Warm the cream and then stir in the brown sugar and cinnamon until both are dissolved. Set aside and let it cool down to room temperature before using.

Cream Cheese Icing

Beat the cream cheese and butter together until smooth. Add the lemon juice, and then the icing sugar. Refrigerate until needed.

<u>Assembly</u>

1. Once the dough is finished, transfer it to a lightly floured counter and roll it out into an 18x24-inch rectangle. You don't have to be precise here.
2. Spread the cinnamon filling over the dough, and then roll the whole thing from one of the long ends. Slice into 9 to 12 rolls.
3. Place each roll into a large, greased pan, leaving room for them to expand. You might need to use two pans.
4. If you're going to bake them tomorrow, cover them with plastic wrap and pop them into the fridge. An hour before you're ready to bake them, let them sit in a warm, draft-free spot for about an hour or until they double in size.
5. Preheat the oven to 350°F.
6. While the oven is heating, pour the room temperature caramel sauce over the rolls.
7. Bake for 20 to 30 minutes or until golden brown. Serve these as they are or go ahead and drizzle with cream cheese icing.

HOT FLASH TIPS

1. *Get outside and get your body moving after eating one of these, or else you'd better grab a blanket because within minutes, you're going to be in a sugar coma on the couch.*
2. *Feel free to add any extras to the cinnamon filling like Plump Raisins* or walnut bits.*
3. *A delicious Cardamon & Banana Filling* is a tasty alternative to the traditional cinnamon filling.*

OVERNIGHT CHICKEN DIJON STRATA

This recipe came from my mom who made it once in the 1980's. I thought it was delicious, but maybe she didn't because we never had it again. If you're not a wine person, you can use chicken broth instead, but I really feel the wine adds a special touch. With layers of sourdough bread, shredded chicken and tasty cheese all baked in a savory egg custard, this dish is perfect for brunch, lunch or dinner. I don't know about you, but I love easy, and preparing this the night before means more time to relax the next day. Take it out of the fridge 30 minutes before baking to speed up the cooking time. Serve with a mixed veggie and fruit salad, and voila! A lovely, balanced meal.

INGREDIENTS

6 cup sourdough bread, cubed
1 cup cooked chicken, shredded
$1/4$ cup green onions, chopped
$1/2$ cup fresh mushrooms, sliced
$1/2$ cup red peppers, diced

3 cup cheese, shredded & divided
8 eggs
$1 1/3$ cup milk
$1/3$ cup dry white wine
2 TB Dijon mustard

DIRECTIONS

1. In a large, greased casserole dish, scatter in the sourdough bread cubes.
2. Over the bread cubes, scatter the chicken, green onions, mushrooms, peppers and 2 C of the cheese.
3. In a large bowl, whisk the eggs, milk, wine and mustard and pour it over the cheese, gently pressing down to make sure everything is well soaked.
4. Top with the remaining 1 C of cheese.
5. Cover and refrigerate overnight.
6. The next morning, uncover and let it rest for 30 minutes before baking.
7. Preheat the oven to 350°F and bake for 45 minutes.
8. Let it sit for about 10 minutes before serving.

HOT FLASH TIP

1. *You can use the entire part of the bread, but if you prefer not to, remove the crusts and use them for Breadcrumbs*.*
2. *You can replace the wine with the same amount of broth if you prefer. And hey, no one's judging if you'd prefer to sip on the wine instead of putting it into the Strata.*

PUMPKIN GLORY MUFFINS

When I go to a new coffee shop, I'm looking for two things: really good coffee and big healthy muffins. You see, muffins have always been my thing. I love to make them, love to eat them and am always looking for new ways to make them healthier while still tasting delicious. I hope you enjoy these muffins because they're bursting with all the warm, cozy flavors of fall, but are light in processed sugar. Score! One of these bad boys will hit the spot with a big ol' mug of something hot. See what I did right there? I'm a poet and I didn't know it.

INGREDIENTS

- 1/4 cup butter, softened
- 1/3 cup brown sugar
- 2 eggs
- 1/2 cup canned pumpkin puree
- 1 1/2 tsp Pumpkin Pie Spice*
- 1/2 tsp ground ginger
- 1/2 tsp maple extract
- 1/2 tsp sea salt

- 1 cup grated carrots
- 1/3 cup crushed pineapple, juice drained
- 1/2 cup Plump Raisins*
- 1/2 cup walnut crumbles
- 1/2 cup shredded coconut
- 1 1/2 cup all-purpose flour
- 1 tsp baking powder
- 1 tsp baking soda

<u>Garnish (optional)</u>

pumpkin seeds, walnut crumbles, or shredded coconut

DIRECTIONS

1. Preheat the oven to 375°F and grease a 12-cup muffin pan.
2. In a large bowl, whisk the butter, brown sugar and eggs together.
3. Stir in pumpkin, pumpkin pie spice, ginger, maple extract and salt.
4. Add carrots, pineapple, raisins, walnuts and coconut and mix well.
5. Fold in flour, baking powder and baking soda.

6. Fill each muffin cup and sprinkle with pumpkin seeds, walnut crumbles, coconut or leave them plain.
7. Bake for 15-18 minutes or until a toothpick inserted in the center comes out clean.

HOT FLASH TIPS

1. *Don't use shriveled raisins! Plump Raisins* are far better in the finished result and so easy to do. Simply soak them in some boiling water for a few minutes before mixing them into your baking.*
2. *Toasted Nuts* add a more flavorful experience to any recipe. Be sure to check out the Odds & Sods section for simple instructions on how to do this.*
3. *Don't have Pumpkin Pie Spice*? Mix 1 tsp cinnamon and 1/4 tsp allspice together, and now you do!*

SAUSAGE & EGG STUFFED CROISSANTS

I love a good weekend brunch, don't you? I don't always want to go out to a restaurant for it though. Most times, I just want to lounge around in my jammies with Jack Johnson or Nora Jones playing in the background, sipping a big cup of java while making a yummy meal. These croissants are filled with cheesy scrambled eggs and homemade sausage. Oh my, so decadent! Because you're saving money by eating at home, splurge and buy some good quality flaky, buttery croissants. Trust me, you will notice the difference. Serve these with fresh-cut fruit or a little fruit salad drizzled with sweetened condensed milk. Luxurious!

INGREDIENTS

6 big croissants, sliced in half

12 eggs

$1/2$ tsp sea salt

$1/4$ tsp white or black pepper

1 TB green onions, finely chopped

1 cup cheddar cheese, shredded

Sausage Patties*

DIRECTIONS

1. Cover a large baking sheet with parchment paper (you might need to use two pans) and put the croissants on with the cut sides up.

2. In a large frying pan, scramble the eggs with salt and pepper until just set, being cautious to not overcook them. Remove from the heat and stir in the green onions and cheese. Cover and set aside.

3. Assembly time! Place the croissants under the broiler for a few seconds until they're lightly toasted. Watch them carefully so they don't burn.

4. Divide the scrambled eggs between each bottom half of the croissants, top with two sausage patties each and then put the top half of the croissant on.

5. Voila!

HOT FLASH TIPS

1. *Nothing beats homemade Sausage Patties*! Make them ahead of time with my recipe under Odds & Sods to make these croissants more easily.*
2. *Feeling a little saucy? Drizzle these stuffed croissants with warm Hollandaise Sauce* and a little sprinkle of smoked paprika.*

SAVORY CHEESE SCONES

These rich and tasty savory cheese scones are perfect for breakfast, lunch or dinner. Enjoy them just as they are, serve with scrambled eggs and fresh fruit, or split them in half for delicious eggs benny. Feel free to add extras to the batter like smoky paprika, chopped chives or even small pieces of ham or bacon.

INGREDIENTS

2 cups all-purpose flour

1 TB baking powder

$1/2$ tsp sea salt

$1/2$ tsp garlic powder

$1/2$ tsp rosemary

$1/2$ cup butter

1 cup cheese, grated (I use aged cheddar)

1 egg

$3/4$ cup Buttermilk*

DIRECTIONS

1. Pre-heat the oven to 425°F.
2. Whisk the flour, baking powder, salt, garlic and rosemary together.
3. Crumble in the butter until it resembles coarse crumbs, and then stir in the cheese.
4. Beat the egg with the buttermilk and stir it into the flour mixture. I use my hands to bring everything together. So satisfying.
5. Using a $1/2$ C measuring cup or a large spoon, drop the dough onto a parchment-lined baking sheet about 2 inches apart. Gently shape them to bring in any straggly bits, but you do want them to look rustic.
6. Bake for 12 to 14 minutes or until golden. Every oven is different, so be mindful of the time.
7. Remove them from the oven and transfer to a cooling rack.
8. Optional: brush the hot scones with garlic butter and sprinkle with a bit of rosemary.

HOT FLASH TIP

1. *If you don't have Buttermilk* hanging out in your fridge, you can easily make it yourself with my recipe in the Odds & Sods section.*

Soups, Salads & Sandwiches

*At its essence, food is nourishing. There is truth in that.
The trick is understanding and respecting the line where it crosses over into something unhealthy.*

—Ashley Graham

ARUGULA SALAD WITH CREAMY CHAMPAGNE DRESSING

Sometimes the simplest of things are the best of things, like this arugula salad with its sunshiny dressing that will have you doing the happy dance and wanting to lick the salad bowl. Yup, it's that good! Since arugula, otherwise known as garden rocket, is part of the mustard greens family, you might notice a hint of a fresh peppery taste, which pairs well with my sweet Creamy Champagne Dressing*. In our house this makes 2 to 3 side salads that we generally serve with BBQ burgers, pizza or grilled cheese sandwiches.

INGREDIENTS

Salad
6 cups arugula greens
$1/2$ English cucumber, thinly sliced
1 cups blueberries
$1/4$ red onion, thinly sliced into slivers
$1/4$ cup sunflower seeds

Creamy Champagne Dressing*
$1/4$ cup champagne vinegar
1 TB freshly squeezed Lemon Juice*
$1/3$ cup good quality olive oil
1 TB yellow mustard
2 TB maple syrup
1 garlic clove, minced
$1/4 - 1/2$ tsp sea salt

DIRECTIONS

1. Whisk all the salad dressing ingredients together and set aside.
2. Toss the arugula with the dressing.
3. Put the salad onto individual plates and top with cucumbers, blueberries and onion.
4. Garnish with sunflower seeds.

HOT FLASH TIPS

1. *This salad will go soggy if you have any leftovers, so eat up, my friend.*
2. *It's easy to turn this into a complete meal by doubling up on the ingredients and adding extras for protein and to make it more filling, such as hemp hearts, edamame beans, tofu or chicken.*

EAST COAST SEAFOOD CHOWDER

Being from the east coast of Canada, chowder was a mainstay in our house and this is how my mom used to make it. She would always serve it with warm biscuits, but it's also great with a thick slice of really good sourdough bread. Since my dad was a lobster fisherman, that's what we used most of the time, but it's delicious with any combination of seafood. I'm not sure why, but I love this even better the next day.

INGREDIENTS

- 1/2 cup onions, diced
- 1/2 cup celery, diced
- 2 strips of thick bacon, diced
- 2 cups low sodium chicken broth
- 1 1/2 cups potatoes, diced
- 1/2 cup carrots, diced
- 1 cup heavy cream
- 1/4 tsp sea salt
- 1/4 tsp white pepper
- 1 cup clams, cooked
- 1 cup prawns, cooked

DIRECTIONS

1. Add the chicken broth, potatoes and carrots, and simmer until all the veggies are tender.
2. Stir in the cream, salt, pepper, clams and shrimp. Let it come to a gentle simmer until you're ready to eat it, but don't let it boil.
3. The longer you let it simmer, the more the flavors get to mingle before you indulge in this creamy chowder.

HOT FLASH TIP

1. *You can experiment with any seafood you like, such as lobster!*
2. *Dill and or tarragon are tasty seasonings to add to this chowder, so feel free to experiment with them.*

KALE & BULGUR SALAD WITH BALSAMIC VINAIGRETTE

This is one of those salads that has evolved over the years. We eat it a lot and are always adding more things to it depending on what we feel like and what's in season. It's a great vegetarian meal, but you can also serve it with grilled chicken, fish, crispy fried tofu or tempeh.

INGREDIENTS

Salad

6 cups kale leaves, shredded (no stems)

$1/2$ cup bulgur, cooked

$1/4$ red onion, diced

1 carrot, shredded

1 medium red pepper, diced

1 medium yellow pepper, diced

1 jalapeño pepper, seeded & chopped

$1/2$ cup cilantro, chopped

1 apple, seeded & diced

$1/2$ cup dried cranberries

$1/2$ cup edamame beans

$1/2$ cup black beans

Garnish

feta or blue cheese crumbles

Toasted Nuts* walnuts or sunflower seeds

Balsamic Vinaigrette*

$1/8$ cup good quality olive oil

$1/4$ cup white balsamic vinegar

2 tsp freshly squeezed Lemon Juice*

1 TB maple syrup

2 tsp chives, chopped

$1/4$ tsp dried rosemary

1 garlic clove, minced

salt & pepper to taste

DIRECTIONS

1. Place all salad ingredients (except the garnish) in a large bowl.
2. In a separate bowl, whisk the vinaigrette ingredients together.
3. Toss the dressing with the salad and place on individual plates.
4. Just before serving, garnish with cheese crumbles and nuts.

HOT FLASH TIP

1. *Kale is a super nutrient-dense vegetable that holds up really well when sitting in a dressing, unlike other greens that can get soggy. It's chock-full of antioxidants to help boost your immune system, chlorophyll to help protect your body from disease and highly absorbable calcium, which is important for bone and muscle health. Eat your kale; it's good for you.*

MAMMA G'S POTATO SALAD

No one has ever made a potato salad like my mother did. It's so good I really didn't change much from the original recipe. Even though we cut back on the amount of fat in this salad, it's still creamy and delicious. It pairs wonderfully with anything grilled on the BBQ or you can serve it over a bed of greens along with sweet little cherry tomatoes.

INGREDIENTS

3 lb Yukon Gold potatoes, diced
4 eggs, hard boiled
$1/2$ cup mayonnaise
$1/2$ cup plain 0% Greek yogurt
1 TB dill pickle liquid (from the jar of pickles)
1 tsp mustard
$1/4$ cup red onion, diced

$1/4$ cup dill pickles, chopped
$3/4$ cup frozen peas, thawed

<u>Garnish</u>

paprika
black pepper
chives, chopped

DIRECTIONS

1. Cook the potatoes until just tender, but not mushy. Drain the water.
2. Chop up 3 of the eggs. Slice the last egg to use as garnish and set aside.
3. In a large bowl, combine the mayonnaise, yogurt, dill pickle liquid and mustard. Add the potatoes, chopped eggs, red onion, pickles and peas. Gently stir everything together until well combined.
4. There is no salt in this recipe, so if you feel it needs a bit, add it now. Refrigerate until you are ready to serve.
5. Before serving, put it into a clean bowl, lay the sliced egg on top and sprinkle with fresh-cracked pepper, paprika and chives.

HOT FLASH TIP

1. *If your potatoes turn out mushy, turn this recipe into just-as-delicious, mashed potato salad!*

OPEN-FACED TUNA SALAD CHEESE BUNS

You might know these as tuna melts, and you may have grown up on them like I did. It was a terrific way to use up leftover hamburger or hot dog buns and was a filling, economical meal, which we ate with carrot sticks and sweet pickles. My kids loved cheese buns, so we started making them this way and it was a big hit. But what sets these apart from your typical tuna melt is the jazzed-up tuna salad.

INGREDIENTS

cheese buns
gruyere cheese, shredded

<u>Tuna Salad</u>
1 can of tuna, drained
1 – 2 tsp Lemon & Dill Dry Spice Mix*
3 TB mayo
$1/2$ apple, finely diced
1 celery stalk, finely diced

DIRECTIONS

1. Mix all the tuna salad ingredients together and spread evenly onto toasted cheese buns.
2. Top each with shredded gruyere cheese and place them under the broiler until melted.

HOT FLASH TIPS

1. In place of tuna, you could opt for a can of drained crab meat. Add 2 chopped hard boiled eggs to the mix.
2. For a little heat, add diced jalapeño peppers.
3. Add a slice of tomato under the cheese to really oomf it up.

ROASTED BROCCOLI SANDWICH

First let me say, I absolutely love roasted broccoli and I can often be found eating a plate of it along with some potatoes any time of the day. In my family, I'm well known for really enjoying the "crispy bits," otherwise known as "charring," or what my husband calls "overdone or burned." But come on, they're the tastiest parts!

Any who, I digress. Let's get into this sandwich, which my husband and son also really enjoy. You can't go wrong with toasted ciabatta buns spread with soft cream cheese, chutney and layered with crispy Roasted Broccoli* and Pickled Red Onions*.

There are no real measurements here, my friend, but one head of broccoli normally gives me 3 or 4 sandwiches.

INGREDIENTS

roasted broccoli
ciabatta buns
cream cheese spread
mango, apple chutney or your favorite chutney
Pickled Red Onions*

Roasted Broccoli*

1 head of broccoli, trimmed & separated into florets
1 TB oil
2 TB freshly squeezed Lemon Juice*
2 TB honey
$1/2$ tsp sea salt
2 cloves garlic, thinly sliced

DIRECTIONS

1. In a large bowl with a lid, gently toss the broccoli florets with the oil, lemon juice, honey, salt and garlic. Alternatively, just get your hands in there because that's pretty satisfying.
2. Preheat your air fryer to 400°F and set the timer for 8 minutes.
3. Once it's preheated, add your broccoli to the basket.
4. When your machine tells you to flip your food, just get in there and give the broccoli a little toss.

5. Toast the buns and spread each side with the cream cheese spread and a little chutney.
6. On the bottom bun, add roasted broccoli and pickled red onions.
7. Put the top bun on, and voila!

HOT FLASH TIPS
1. *Don't have an air fryer? Roast the broccoli in the oven instead. Toss the broccoli with the same ingredients. Put everything on a parchment-lined baking sheet and roast at 400°F for about 25 minutes or until they're starting to brown.*
2. *You can pair this with a salad of mixed greens, sliced red peppers, sliced cucumbers, red onions, blueberries and drizzle it all with my Creamy Champagne Vinaigrette*. Just like that, you've got yourself a lovely vegetarian meal.*

ROASTED BUTTERNUT SQUASH SOUP

A delicious, creamy soup that's filling without all the added fat? Yes, please! Roasting the veggies together before pureeing them in the blender makes this an easy peasy soup to put together. Serve this with toasted sourdough spread with hummus and Pickled Red Onions* or stir it into cooked noodles topped with crumbled croutons and serve with Roasted Broccoli*.

INGREDIENTS

1 medium butternut squash, peeled, seeded & cubed
1 medium yellow onion, peeled & cut into quarters
4 whole garlic cloves, peeled
1 TB olive oil
1 TB white balsamic vinegar
1 cup canned low sodium white beans, drained

3 cups low sodium chicken broth
1 TB tomato paste
1 tsp rosemary
1 tsp sage
$1/2$ tsp smoked paprika
$1/2$ cup light cream
1 TB freshly grated parmesan cheese

Garnish
parsley, chopped
pepitas, roasted
croutons
parmesan cheese
yogurt

DIRECTIONS

1. Preheat the oven to 425°F and line a large baking sheet with parchment paper.
2. Toss the squash, onion, garlic, oil and vinegar together and spread them out onto the baking sheet.
3. Roast for about 30 minutes or until veggies look brown and caramelized.
4. Transfer the veggies to a blender, along with the beans, chicken broth, tomato paste, and spices. Process it until smooth.

5. Pour the soup into a large saucepan. Add the cream and parmesan cheese, and simmer until the soup is heated through.
6. Garnish with chopped parsley, roasted pepitas, croutons, a sprinkle of parmesan or a dollop of yogurt.

HOT FLASH TIPS

1. *To safely cut a butternut squash: Remember, it's always easier to cut something that has a flat surface and doesn't slide around. First, slice off the bottom and top of the squash and stand it upright. Putting pressure on the knife handle and the top of the blade, slice straight down the center to the bottom.*
2. *Leftover tomato paste? Using a 1 T measuring spoon, spoon the paste into an ice cube tray and freeze. Once frozen, pop them out and store in a freezer-safe container.*
3. *"Beans, beans, they're good for your heart…" For the average healthy person, it's a good idea to get more beans and legumes into your diet but be sure to introduce them slowly and drink plenty of water. They can bloat your tummy and make you gassy until your body adjusts to them.*
4. *When I'm out of my homemade dry Breadcrumbs*, I put a handful of tasty croutons into a little food processor and pulse until they're the texture I like. You can keep them in a container and use them whenever you feel like having some crumbs on top of your soup, noodles or roasted veggies.*

SPINACH & FETA TURKEY BURGERS

With our love of Mediterranean food, I decided to add a few of our favorite ingredients to our plain turkey burgers one day, and holy moly! The addition of spinach, briny feta cheese and Fresh Basil Pesto* took these to a new level of deliciousness. Serve these on fresh buns and load up on all the yummy things, like seared back bacon, Pickled Red Onions*, soft butter lettuce, arugula, cucumber, tomato, olive tapenade or a drizzle of Greek Tzatziki Sauce*.

INGREDIENTS

2 lbs lean ground turkey or chicken

1 cup spinach or kale, finely chopped

1/2 cup crumbled low fat feta cheese

1/2 cup Breadcrumbs* or Oat Flour*

2 TB Basil Pesto*

DIRECTIONS

1. In a large bowl, mix all ingredients together.
2. Divide into 6 patties and place them on a parchment-lined plate. Let them chill in the fridge for at least 60 minutes.
3. Heat up the grill and BBQ them just like you would any burger or panfry them until brown on both sides and the juices run clear.

HOT FLASH TIPS

1. *Top your burger with my Greek Tzatziki Sauce* and pair with a simple arugula or Greek salad.*
2. *In this recipe, you can choose between Breadcrumbs* or Oat Flour*, but these two ingredients are not always interchangeable, so keep that in mind with other recipes that call for one or the other.*

Comfort Foods

Winter blues are cured every time with a potato gratin paired with a roast chicken.

—Alexandra Guarnaschelli

BAKED MAC & CHEESE

Baked mac and cheese sure brings back memories, doesn't it? This recipe fills a large baking pan, so you can have lots of leftovers. Now, let me tell you, this is so good that once you mix the sauce with the noodles, you're going to want to eat it right away. Hey, no one's going to fault you for that—this stuff is crazy delicious. But if you're like me and love a buttery crumb on top, follow the recipe to the end. Serve this with a tossed salad or roasted veggies, and you've got yourself a lovely balanced meal.

INGREDIENTS

2 cups dry macaroni, cooked and drained
extra yummy bits (optional, see Hot Flash Tips below)

Bread Crumb Topping
1 1/2 cups panko breadcrumbs
1/3 cup butter, melted
1 garlic clove, finely minced
1/2 tsp garlic powder

Sauce
2 cups light cream
1/4 cup all-purpose flour
1/2 tsp dry mustard powder
1/2 tsp onion powder
1/4 tsp white pepper
1/2 tsp sea salt
2 cups cheddar cheese, shredded

DIRECTIONS

1. Preheat the oven to 375°F.
2. In a large saucepan, whisk the cream, flour, mustard, onion, pepper and salt together. Cook over medium heat, stirring constantly until thickened.
3. Stir in the cheese and continue stirring until melted.
4. Add the cooked and drained macaroni noodles and give it all a good toss. If you're using the extra yummies bits, add them now.
5. Lightly grease a 9x13 baking dish and fill it with the macaroni and cheese mixture.
6. Make the crumble by mixing the breadcrumbs with the melted butter, minced garlic and garlic powder. Crumble it over the macaroni.
7. Bake for 10 to 15 minutes or until the crumbs are golden.

HOT FLASH TIP

1. Extra yummy bits added to the sauce will make this recipe over-the-top delicious! I like to use $1/2$ C chopped real bacon bits or slices of cooked chorizo sausage.
2. For a little more nutritional value, add $1/4$ C hemp hearts to the crumb mixture.
3. Did you know you can substitute ground hemp heart flour for all-purpose flour when coating chicken or tofu? Delicious and nutritious!

BASIL PESTO PIZZA

I have always loved pizza, and when our kids were growing up, Friday night meant pizza night. Sometimes we had takeout, but most often, it was so much fun to make our own and create great memories together. Even though we don't have pizza every Friday night anymore, there's still this little something inside me that says, "Ooh, it's Friday night—pizza!" I'm sure I could write an entire book just on pizza, but I'll just share a few of our favorites with you, and maybe you can start creating some fun pizza memories with your family.

I'll never forget the very first pizza pie I ever had with my grandmother. It was a simple cheese pizza on a beautiful soft chewy crust. Today, I still love a simple cheese pizza, but instead of tomato sauce, I really enjoy using Basil Pesto*. Other than that, I like to keep it simple, but you could add thin slices of tomato or fresh basil leaves for an extra little pop on top.

INGREDIENTS

Pizza Dough*

1/3 cup Basil Pesto*

1 – 2 cups mozzarella cheese, grated

DIRECTIONS

1. Preheat the oven to 475°F.
2. Stretch the dough into a rustic shape on a sheet or pizza pan and prebake in the oven for 5 minutes.
3. Remove it from the oven, spread the prebaked dough with basil pesto and top with cheese. If you want to add sliced tomatoes, do it now.
4. Return your pizza to the oven and bake for another 10 minutes or until bubbly.

HOT FLASH TIPS

1. *If you prefer, you could use my 3-Cheese Blend* instead of the plain mozzarella.*
2. *Instead of grated cheese, you could cut the cheese—er, I mean slice it—and lay the pieces on.*
3. *You could also add any toppings you want, but I like to keep mine pretty simple.*

BBQ CHICKEN PIZZA WITH CREAMY RANCH DRESSING

This is one of those drool-worthy, finger-licking deliciouspizzas that you just can't stop eating. Make sure to use a super tasty BBQ sauce. You want just the right sweetness to pull this off.

INGREDIENTS

Homemade Pizza Dough*

1/2 cup BBQ sauce

2 cups cooked chicken, shredded

1/4 red onion, sliced into thin strips

1/2 cup pineapple chunks

1/2 cup cherry tomatoes, quartered

2 cups mozzarella cheese, grated

Creamy Ranch Dressing*

DIRECTIONS

1. Preheat the oven to 475°F.
2. Stretch the pizza dough into a rustic shape on a sheet pan or pizza pan and pre-bake in the oven for 5 minutes.
3. Toss the chicken with the BBQ sauce and spread over the prebaked dough.
4. Cover with grated cheese.
5. Top with onion, pineapple and tomatoes.
6. Bake for another 10 minutes or until the cheese is bubbling and the edges of the crust are golden brown.
7. Drizzle with my creamy ranch dressing.

HOT FLASH TIPS

1. *I love this recipe with a sweet and smoky BBQ sauce like Stubbs or Sweet Baby Ray's.*
2. *My Creamy Ranch Dressing* is lower in fat and sodium than the store-bought alternative, plus it's freshly made and absolutely delicious.*
   You could also try this with my 3-Cheese Blend* instead of the plain mozzarella.

BEEF STROGANOFF

My husband is of German descent, and stroganoff is definitely comfort food in our house. Over the years, we discovered this dish is so much better when you use a higher quality steak that has a good amount of marbling throughout it. Pan searing the meat first gives it a beautiful, rich, deep flavor. The sauce is equally delicious served over hot buttery egg noodles or creamy garlic mashed potatoes. I would serve this simple dish with peas and carrots, tossed salad and warm buns.

INGREDIENTS

1 lb rib eye steaks
1/2 tsp sea salt
1/4 tsp white pepper
1/2 tsp garlic powder
1 medium yellow onion, sliced
2 cups fresh mushrooms, quartered
1/4 cup dry red wine
2 cups low sodium beef broth

1 tsp grainy Dijon mustard
1 tsp Worcestershire sauce
1/2 tsp smoked paprika
3 TB all-purpose flour
1 cup sour cream or Greek yogurt
cooked egg noodles or creamy garlic mashed potatoes
2 tsp dried parsley

DIRECTIONS

1. Slice the steaks into strips and sprinkle them lightly with salt, pepper and garlic.

2. For the best results, I use a glazed cast-iron pan. Place it over high heat and once it gets hot, add a touch of oil and then carefully place the steak pieces in the pan. Let them sear until well browned. If you have a splatter screen, use it. Once seared, remove and place them on a platter.

3. Turn the heat down to medium-low, add the onion, mushrooms and wine. Cover and let the veggies cook down.

4. Uncover and stir in the broth, mustard, Worcestershire and paprika. Let this cook over medium-low heat for about 5 minutes.

5. Whisk the flour into the sour cream or yogurt and then stir it into the pan until it's well mixed.

6. Add the beef and give it a stir. Remove the pan from the heat.

7. Serve over hot noodles or creamy garlic potatoes and sprinkle with parsley.

HOT FLASH TIP

1. *The better the rib eye, the better the stroganoff. Trust me, you want good quality here, my friend.*

CHICKEN STEW WITH FLUFFY DUMPLINGS

Growing up on the east coast of Canada, we had our fair share of stew and dumplings. It was a cheap and easy meal, but also full of flavor and comfort. I still use the same dumpling recipe my mom used to make, but I have added lemon to it because lemon just goes so well with chicken. This stew is rich and creamy and tastes really good the next day. I serve this with warm, lightly buttered biscuits.

INGREDIENTS

<u>Stew</u>
2 TB butter
1 large onion, diced
2 large carrots, diced
3 stalks of celery, diced
4 cups low sodium chicken broth
$1/2$ cup light cream
$1/4$ cup all-purpose flour
3 cups chicken, chopped
1 tsp Poultry Seasoning*

1 cup frozen peas
<u>Dumplings</u>
$1 1/3$ cups all-purpose flour
2 tsp baking powder
$1/2$ tsp sea salt
1 tsp Lemon Zest*
$2/3$ cup milk
1 tsp freshly squeezed Lemon Juice*

DIRECTIONS

<u>Dumplings</u>

1. Whisk the flour, baking powder, salt and lemon zest together in a medium bowl.
2. In a separate bowl, stir the milk and lemon juice together.
3. Very gently, mix the milk mixture into the dry ingredients, just until it comes together.
4. Let the dough sit while preparing the stew.

<u>Stew</u>

1. In a large soup pot, sauté the onions, carrots and celery in the butter for about 5 minutes until the veggies have softened.

2. Add the chicken broth and turn the heat down to a gentle simmer.
3. In a bowl, whisk the cream with the flour, and then stir it into the soup pot.
4. Add the chicken, poultry seasoning and peas.
5. Once the stew has returned to a gentle simmer, quickly drop balls of the dumpling dough on top of the hot stew using a 1 T measure.
6. Cover and do not lift the lid for 18 minutes while they're steaming. This is the magic that makes the dumplings fluffy.
7. Serve and enjoy!

HOT FLASH TIPS

1. *The dumplings will double in size, so be mindful of that.*
2. *No peeking under the lid while the dumplings are steaming. If you don't have a glass lid, now might be the time to invest in one.*
3. *If you don't have Poultry Seasoning*, use a $1/2$ tsp dried sage and $1/2$ tsp thyme.*

CREAMY PESTO PASTA WITH TURKEY MEATBALLS

Nothing says comfort food more than creamy pasta and tender meatballs on a chilly night. I love Basil Pesto*, so it just made sense to add it to our meatballs because I've been putting it into our pasta and on our pizza for as long as I can remember.

INGREDIENTS

<u>Meatballs</u>
1 lb ground turkey
2 TB Basil Pesto*
1 green onion, finely diced
$1/2$ tsp sea salt
1 tsp garlic powder
$3/4$ cup panko breadcrumbs

<u>Pasta</u>
2 cups dried penne noodles
1 cup Basil Pesto*
$1/2$ cup light cream
$1/4$ tsp salt
$1/4$ tsp pepper
reserved pasta water, as needed

<u>Garnish</u>
basil or parsley, chopped
parmesan cheese

DIRECTIONS

1. Preheat the oven to 425°F.
2. Gently mix the meatball ingredients together and form into balls using a 2 T scoop or just eyeball it.
3. Place them on a baking sheet covered with parchment paper, a stone baking pan or a glazed cast-iron skillet.
4. Bake for 30 to 45 minutes or until they're cooked through and browned.
5. While the meatballs are roasting, cook the noodles, drain (remember to reserve some of the water) and put the noodles back into the pot.
6. Stir in the basil pesto, cream, salt, and pepper. Turn the burner on medium-low and just cook until heated through. Once it's hot, remove from the heat and

cover until the meatballs are cooked. If the sauce seems too thick, add a bit of pasta water.

7. Serve the meatballs over the pasta and garnish with freshly chopped basil or parsley and a little sprinkle of freshly grated parmesan cheese.

HOT FLASH TIP

1. *This pairs perfectly with my fresh and simple Arugula Salad* and maybe a thick slice of sourdough bread.*

Comfort Foods

FRENCH ACADIAN RAPPIE PIE

I was a little hesitant to include this recipe because it's a labor of love and one that even we only make once a year for a special occasion. Rappie pie, or *râpure* in French, is one of our French Acadian soul food dishes that has been passed down from generation to generation by the French homesteaders in Nova Scotia.

Back then, potatoes were plentiful and the meat in the pie varied due to whatever game they could hunt. The potatoes were grated by hand and all of the liquid squeezed out until the potatoes were dry.

In certain parts of Nova Scotia today, you can purchase large blocks of frozen grated potato that have the liquid already removed. Since I don't have access to that where we live currently, I use a modern-day convenience—the juicer. I'm sure my great-great-grandmothers would have loved it!

INGREDIENTS

$3/4$ cup butter, melted & divided

2 whole chickens, or 2 lb chicken thighs, cooked

12 cups chicken broth (might not use it all)

1 large onion, diced

salt & pepper

5 lb potatoes, peeled & grated

DIRECTIONS

1. Pour $1/2$ C of the melted butter into a deep-dish baking pan and set aside until you're ready to assemble everything. If you don't have one large pan, use two smaller ones.

2. Discard the skin, fat and bones from the cooked chickens, shred the meat and set it aside.

3. Pour the chicken broth, onion and remaining $1/4$ C of butter into a large pot. Bring it to a boil, then reduce the heat to a low simmer. Cover and keep it on a low simmer while you prepare the potatoes. You want the onions to get almost translucent and very soft.

4. Juice all the potatoes, picking out any large chunks that didn't go through the juicer. Put the potatoes in one large bowl, and the starchy liquid into a measuring cup. Take note of how much liquid came out of the potatoes because that will let you know how much chicken broth you will need.

5. You will see the potato starch settle to the bottom of the measuring cup. You will also want to take note of how much starch there is because you will be adding half of it into the hot chicken broth.

Assembly

1. Measure the same amount of hot broth as the liquid you got out of the potatoes. Working quickly and using a strong wooden spoon, stir about 2 C of broth at a time into the potatoes. Once stirred really well, add another 2 C, and so on until you've added all you're supposed to. You will feel the potato mixture becoming gelatinous and thick.

2. Pour half of the hot potato mixture into the prepared pan. Top it with all of the chicken. Give it a sprinkling of sea salt, a few grinds of black pepper and then pour the remaining potato mixture over the top.

3. Smooth it out and bake at 450°F for 45 minutes. Turn the heat down to 350°F and continue to bake for another 2 to $2^{1}/_{2}$ hours or until golden brown and crisp.

HOT FLASH TIP

1. *We serve ours with a little butter, a sprinkle of salt and pepper and a spoonful of pickled green tomato chow-chow or fancy molasses. I recommend trying the chow-chow by Graves, Habitant and Compliments.*

2. *To cook the whole chickens like they would have done in the old days, put them in a large pot of salted water along with lots of cut up onions, celery, carrots, sage and rosemary leaves. After it cooks, separate the meat from the bones and strain the broth for future use.*

SHEET PAN LEMON CHICKEN & ROSEMARY POTATOES

Can you say easy peasy lemon squeezy? We love sheet pan meals, and this one is made extra special using Lemon Curd*, rosemary and garlic, which is all tucked under the skin. Once baked, you can turn the broiler on for a few minutes to get the skin extra crispy.

INGREDIENTS

2 TB garlic powder
2 tsp dried rosemary
1 tsp sea salt
$1/4$ tsp black pepper

4 boneless chicken thighs, or small boneless breasts with skin still attached
4 TB Lemon Curd*
1 – 2 TB butter, melted
2 lb potatoes, quartered
1 – 2 TB olive or avocado oil

DIRECTIONS

1. Preheat the oven to 425°F.
2. In a small bowl, combine the garlic powder, rosemary, salt and pepper.
3. On one side of a parchment-lined baking sheet, place the chicken pieces skin-side up.
4. Loosen the skin and spoon some of the lemon curd over the meat. Sprinkle some of the dried herbs onto the lemon curd and pat the skin back in place. The remaining herbs will go on the potatoes.
5. Lightly spread each chicken piece with melted butter and a sprinkle of sea salt.
6. In a large bowl, toss the cut potatoes with the remaining herbs and the oil. Spread them out on the other side of the sheet pan.
7. Bake for 45 minutes or until the chicken is cooked through and the potatoes are tender.

HOT FLASH TIP

1. *We like to serve this with steamed asparagus drizzled with fresh Lemon Juice* and freshly grated parmesan cheese.*

THE BEST POTATO GRATIN

Stop looking for the best potato gratin recipe because you've just found it. I'm not holding anything back here, my friend! Thinly sliced potatoes, heavy cream and tasty cheese all baked until golden brown and bubbly. Oh My Gosh…so simple, so delicious.

INGREDIENTS

8 cups (2½ lb bag) Yukon Gold or russet potatoes, sliced

2 TB butter, softened

1 tsp salt

½ tsp white pepper

2 cups Asiago cheese

2 cups heavy whipping cream (33%)

DIRECTIONS

1. Preheat the oven to 325°F.
2. Peel and thinly slice the potatoes using a mandolin or food processor. If you have a nice steady hand and can make about ⅛-inch slices, you can do it manually.
3. Grease an oven-safe skillet with the softened butter and layer the potatoes, making sure to season each layer with a little pinch of salt, pepper and cheese.
4. After the last layer of potatoes, pour the cream evenly over the top.
5. Cover and bake for 90 minutes.
6. After 90 minutes, increase the heat to 425°F, uncover and continue to bake another 15 minutes or until bubbly, nicely browned and the potatoes feel soft.

HOT FLASH TIP

1. For the best results, use a glazed cast-iron skillet.
2. Slice the potatoes by any method that works for you. The thinner, the better. Make sure they're all uniform in size so they cook evenly.
3. Once finished, let this sit for at least 10 minutes before serving to allow things to settle.

Sweet Treats

You can be miserable before you have a cookie and you can be miserable after you eat a cookie but you can't be miserable while you are eating a cookie.

—Ina Garten

APPLE CRUMBLE

I've been making apple crumble for so long that I can make it without a recipe, you know what I mean? So, when I decided to add it to this recipe book, I actually had to go back and figure out how much of everything went into it. The crumble is the tricky part because I find most other crumbles too dry. There must be the perfect balance of butter, sugar and flour. I know I nailed it because this one turns out perfectly every time. One of the little tricks I discovered over the years is to cook the apples down a little bit because then you can get more of the crumble on top. This is so yummy served as a dessert with ice cream or go ahead and have it for breakfast with vanilla yogurt. Absolutely scrumptious!

INGREDIENTS

<u>Filling</u>
5 lb bag of McIntosh apples or any other soft, sweet apple
1/4 cup water
1 – 2 TB brown sugar
2 tsp cinnamon
1/4 tsp nutmeg

<u>Crumble</u>
1/2 cup dark brown sugar
1 tsp cinnamon
1/2 cup butter, softened
1 1/2 cup all-purpose flour
1/2 cup Toasted Nuts* walnut crumbles

DIRECTIONS

1. Preheat the oven to 375°F.
2. Peel and slice the apples and put them into a large saucepan along with the water and brown sugar.
3. Cook over medium heat until the apples have softened but are still holding their shape. Stir in the cinnamon and nutmeg and then pour it into a large baking dish.
4. Prepare the crumble by mixing the brown sugar and cinnamon, and then cut the butter into it. Mix in the flour next, and then the nuts.
5. Using your hand, crumble it evenly over the apple mixture.
6. Bake for 30 minutes or until golden brown and bubbly.

HOT FLASH TIPS

1. *You can easily make a few of these ahead of time. Once the crumble is on, cover it and store in the freezer without baking until you want to enjoy it. To bake from frozen, preheat the oven to 350° F, cover the apple crumble with foil and pop it into the oven for 30 minutes. Uncover and continue to bake for another 20 to 30 minutes or until the apples are bubbling and the topping is golden brown.*

APPLE & STILTON CRUMBLE

If you grew up having a chunk of cheddar with your apple pie like I did, you'll understand why this recipe works so well. If you have no clue what I'm talking about, just trust me on this one. This recipe uses either a pear or ginger stilton, which is a soft, rich and crumbly cheese speckled with bits of pear or candied ginger.

INGREDIENTS

<u>Filling</u>
5 lb bag apples
1 – 2 TB dark brown sugar
$1/4$ cup water
1 TB candied ginger, crumbled

<u>Crumble</u>
$1/3$ cup butter, softened
$1/3$ cup dark brown sugar
1 cup all-purpose flour
$1/3$ cup crumbled pear Stilton cheese
2 TB chopped walnuts or pecans

DIRECTIONS

1. Preheat the oven to 375°F.
2. To make the filling, peel and slice the apples and put them into a large saucepan along with the brown sugar and water.
3. Cook over medium heat until the apples have softened but are still holding their shape. Add the ginger and pour it all into a large baking dish.
4. Prepare the crumble by cutting the softened butter into the brown sugar. Mix in the flour, cheese and nuts. Using your hand, crumble it on top of the apples.
5. Bake for 30 minutes or until the crumble is golden brown.

HOT FLASH TIPS

1. *You can purchase candied or crystalized ginger from most grocery stores. They even carry it in the bulk section.*
2. *You can replace the apples with sliced pears or do a combination of both.*

CANADIAN BUTTER TARTS

I'm a proud Canadian, and one of our sweet treats is the butter tart, a quintessential dessert thought to have originated in Ontario. Every home has their unique way of making them. For years, I played with my mom's recipe and finally got it to the point where we all agreed and liked this version the best. Homemade sweet pastry with a perfectly gooey filling. Yes, you can purchase premade tart shells, but the homemade butter pastry is what makes them so special.

INGREDIENTS

<u>Pastry</u>

1 1/4 cups all-purpose flour
1/2 tsp sea salt
1 tsp sugar
1/2 cup butter, frozen & grated
4 TB ice-cold water

<u>Filling</u>

2 eggs
¼ cup butter, softened
¾ cup brown sugar
½ cup golden corn syrup
1 tsp rum extract
1 cup Plump Raisins*

DIRECTIONS

<u>Pastry</u>

1. Place the flour, salt and sugar in a food processor and give it a few whirls to mix.
2. Add the grated butter and pulse until it looks like coarse sand.
3. Add the water (make sure it's ice cold) and pulse again until the dough starts pulling away from the sides and looks like it's roughly holding itself together.

4. Scoop it out and place on a floured counter. I like to use a sifter because it makes the flour spread out evenly.

5. Shape it into a disk and use a rolling pin to roll it out. Cut out one 3- to 4-inch circle and place it in a muffin tin to make sure it fits properly. Gently press it into the bottom and sides. If it looks good, carry on with the remaining dough, making the same sized circles. There should be enough dough to make 12.

6. Put the muffin pan in the freezer for about 10 minutes. You want the butter to remain as cold as possible, because as it bakes, those little frozen bits of butter are going to burst, creating air pockets, giving you a tender, flaky crust.

Filling & Baking

1. Preheat the oven to 425°F.

2. Lightly whisk the eggs, butter, sugar, corn syrup and extract until creamy. Do not overmix. Overmixing results in the filling separating and a sugary texture on top.

3. Divide the raisins between each tart shell and then pour the filling over each one until it's all used up.

4. Bake for 10 minutes until the crust starts to brown. Reduce temperature to 350°F and continue baking for another 5-7 minutes.

5. Remove them from the oven and let them sit for 5 minutes before loosening from the pan. Transferring them to a cooling rack.

6. Store leftovers in the fridge and bring them to room temperature before serving.

HOT FLASH TIP

1. *When making any pastries, the trick to getting a flaky, tender crumb or crust that holds up well is to use ice cold water and frozen butter.*

2. *If you have a little extra time, take $^1/_4$ C blocks of butter, grate them and store in the freezer for future use.*

3. *This is the perfect time to practice mindful eating. Allow yourself to enjoy one butter tart with zero guilt and have another one tomorrow.*

CHOCOLATE CAKE WITH MARSHMALLOW FROSTING

This is a cake my mother would make for our birthdays that would get lots of oohs and aahs every single time. Maybe it was because she would hide nickels and dimes wrapped in wax paper inside the cake (heaven only knows how we never managed to choke on those coins). The batter is thin, but it bakes up into a heavy, rich cake that could be eaten without frosting, but don't do it. The marshmallow frosting tastes like…well, it tastes like soft delicious marshmallows.

INGREDIENTS

<u>Cake</u>

1 1/2 cups sugar

1/2 cup butter, melted

2 eggs

1/2 cup milk

1 tsp vanilla extract

1/2 cup cocoa

1 cup hot water (you may not use it all)

1 1/2 cup all-purpose flour

1 tsp baking soda

1/2 tsp sea salt

<u>Marshmallow Frosting</u>

1 1/2 cup sugar

6 TB cold water

2 egg whites

1/4 tsp cream of tartar

1/8 tsp sea salt

1 tsp vanilla

DIRECTIONS

<u>Cake</u>

1. Preheat the oven to 350°F and grease a 9x13 pan.
2. Using a hand mixer or stand mixer, cream the sugar and butter together.
3. Add the eggs and beat until light and fluffy.
4. Add the milk and vanilla and mix again.

5. Using a glass measuring cup, spoon the cocoa in and slowly fill to the one cup line with hot water, whisking until there are no lumps. Add this to the bowl and mix all together again.
6. Stir in the flour, baking soda and salt until well combined.
7. Pour into a greased pan and bake for 40 minutes or until a toothpick inserted in the center comes out clean. Let it cool down completely before frosting.

<u>Marshmallow Frosting</u>

1. Using a double boiler, combine the sugar, water, egg whites, cream of tartar and salt (this is going to require patience so relax and focus on your breathing).
2. Using a hand blender, beat the frosting for about 7 minutes or until it reaches stiff shiny peaks.
3. Remove it from the heat and stir in the vanilla.
4. Spread the frosting over the cooled cake.

HOT FLASH TIP

1. *Don't have a double boiler? Just put a smaller pot into a larger one that is half full of boiling water.*
2. *Use the leftover egg yolks to make a Hollandaise Sauce* for dinner or breakfast the next morning.*

LAYERED LEMON CHEESECAKE

Let me tell you, this is one sexy dessert. I mean, come on! A buttery almond crust, topped with creamy cheesecake, topped with lemon pie filling—oh, be still my beating heart! We've been making this dessert since the 1970's, and I just knew it was going to be a star in my recipe book one day. You can make this in a cheesecake pan or a 9x13 pan with equally good results.

INGREDIENTS

Crust
$1/2$ cup butter, softened
2 tsp sugar
1 cup flour
$1/2$ cup finely crushed almonds or almond meal

Cream Cheese Layer
8 oz package light cream cheese, softened
$1/3$ cup Icing Sugar*
$1/2$ tsp vanilla

1 cup Stabilized Whipped Cream*

Lemon Layer
212 g (7.5 oz) box lemon pie filling (you will need to cook it), or a 540 ml (21 oz) can of lemon pie filling

Topping
leftover Stabilized Whipped Cream*

DIRECTIONS

Crust

1. Preheat the oven to 350°F.
2. Prepare the crust by mixing the butter and sugar and then adding the flour and almonds.
3. Pat the crust into a springform pan or a cheesecake pan, whichever one has removable sides.
4. Bake for 12 minutes or until golden. Let it cool on the counter while you're putting the rest of the recipe together.

Cream Cheese Layer

1. Combine the cream cheese, icing sugar and vanilla. Blend until smooth.
2. Using a whisk, fold in the stabilized whipped cream, and then pour it over the cooled crust.
3. Refrigerate for 60 minutes.

Lemon Layer

1. Make the lemon pie filling according to the package directions (if you have a can, you can skip this step).
2. Take the pan out of the refrigerator and pour the lemon filling over the cream cheese mixture, smoothing out the top.
3. Pop it back into the refrigerator to set for a minimum of 60 minutes.

Topping

1. Once everything is set, top it with more stabilized whipped cream and garnish with lemon slices or slivered almonds.

HOT FLASH TIPS

1. For the cream cheese layer, make sure to use Icing Sugar* and not granulated sugar. You need the cornstarch in the icing sugar to help thicken the cheesecake.

OATMEAL CHOCOLATE CHIP COOKIES

If you're looking for a delicious oatmeal chocolate chip cookie with no dairy, refined sugar or flour, here you go! I've been making this recipe for quite a few years, and without fail, I always get nine perfectly sized cookies. If you want some for the freezer, be sure to double this recipe.

INGREDIENTS

1 banana with lots of brown spots on it
1/2 cup natural peanut butter
1/2 cup Date Paste*
1 tsp vanilla or rum extract
1 cup oats

1/2 tsp baking soda
1/8 tsp sea salt
1/3 cup chocolate chips
1/4 cup Toasted Nut* walnut crumbles

DIRECTIONS

1. Preheat the oven to 350°F.
2. Mash the banana with the peanut butter and stir in the date paste and extract.
3. Mix in the oats, baking soda, salt, chocolate chips and nuts.
4. Drop by tablespoonfuls onto a parchment-lined baking sheet.
5. Bake for 18 to 20 minutes.

HOT FLASH TIPS

1. *You get added nutritional benefits when you use Date Paste* instead of granulated sugar.*

SOURDOUGH BREAD PUDDING WITH SWEET RUM SAUCE

When I was growing up, bread pudding was a delicious treat in our house, but it was also a clever way to use up leftover bread. Today, I use day-old sourdough or brioche bread because they hold up perfectly in the lightly spiced, creamy egg custard. Serve it warm from the oven, drizzled with a little Sweet Rum Sauce* and a scoop of vanilla ice cream.

INGREDIENTS

8 slices of thick sourdough bread, cubed

1 cup Plump Raisins*

$1/4$ cup sugar

1 tsp vanilla or rum extract

4 eggs

$1/2$ tsp cinnamon

2 cup milk

$1/4$ tsp nutmeg

Sweet Rum Sauce*

14 oz can sweetened condensed milk

2 TB butter

1 tsp water

1 tsp cornstarch

1 – 2 tsp rum extract

DIRECTIONS

Bread Pudding

1. Preheat the oven to 350°F.
2. Scatter the bread cubes and raisins in a large well-greased casserole dish.
3. Whisk all the remaining ingredients together (except for the sweet rum sauce) and pour it over the bread, making sure it gets well soaked.
4. Cover it with foil and bake for 45 minutes or until a toothpick inserted in the center comes out clean.

Sweet Rum Sauce

1. While the pudding is in the oven, make the sauce.

2. Heat the condensed milk and butter in a saucepan over medium heat until the butter is melted and the mixture is hot.

3. In a bowl, whisk the water, cornstarch and extract together, and then add it into the milk mixture, stirring constantly. Once it comes to a boil, remove it from the heat.

<u>Assembly</u>

Serve the bread pudding with my sweet rum sauce and a little vanilla ice cream.

HOT FLASH TIPS

1. *Drizzle the Sweet Rum Sauce* over fruit salad, baked yams, French toast, pancakes or waffles.*

Odds & Sods

One of the very nicest things about life is the way we must regularly stop whatever it is we are doing and devote our attention to eating.
—Luciano Pavarotti

3-CHEESE BLEND

This is our go-to cheese blend for pizza, lasagna and grilled cheese sandwiches, but feel free to get creative with other flavors of cheese. Yes, you can buy store-bought blends, but they generally have cornstarch or flour added to prevent the cheese from sticking together. It's a personal choice here and there is no right or wrong answer, but I prefer to blend my own where I can have control over what cheeses I use.

INGREDIENTS

4 cups full fat mozzarella, grated
1 cup full fat cheddar, grated
1 cup full fat jack, grated

DIRECTIONS

Combine all three cheeses and use it however you want!

HOT FLASH TIPS

1. If you have any leftover grated cheese, you can sprinkle just a little bit of cornstarch, flour or potato starch to prevent it from sticking together. I find it's better if you store it in a larger container rather than stuffing it into a small one.
2. Feel free to add your own herbs and spices as well, such as an Italian blend, taco or garlic powder.

BALSAMIC VINAIGRETTE

This balsamic dressing is so good on salads, but it's also great on Buddha bowls and pasta salads or drizzled on fish, chicken and roasted veggies.

INGREDIENTS

- $\frac{1}{4}$ cup good quality olive oil
- $\frac{1}{3}$ cup white balsamic vinegar
- 1 TB pure maple syrup
- 1 garlic clove, minced
- $\frac{1}{4}$ tsp sea salt
- $\frac{1}{2}$ tsp chives, chopped
- $\frac{1}{2}$ tsp rosemary, chopped
- $\frac{1}{2}$ tsp Lemon Zest*

DIRECTIONS

Combine all ingredients in a mason jar and shake, shake, shake.

HOT FLASH TIP

1. *You can also use dark balsamic vinegar in place of white. I just love the color when I use the white, but it's a personal preference here, my friend.*
2. *Store this dressing in the fridge but allow it to come to room temperature before using since olive oil will solidify at colder temperatures.*

BREADCRUMBS

Don't waste leftover bread or crusts any longer!

INGREDIENTS

leftover bread or crusts (that's it!)

DIRECTIONS

1. Spread the bread or crusts out onto a sheet pan and bake at 325°F for about 15 minutes or until they're just starting to brown and smell fragrant.
2. Put them in a food processor and pulse until you get the crumb texture you like.
3. Store in an airtight container and use whenever a recipe calls for plain breadcrumbs.

HOT FLASH TIPS

1. *Save money and make your own Italian breadcrumbs. To each cup of crumbs, add $1/2$ tsp oregano, $1/2$ tsp garlic powder, $1/4$ tsp rosemary, $1/8$ tsp onion powder and $1/8$ tsp salt.*

BREAKFAST OATS

Make a big batch of oats to have on hand for a quick and easy breakfast.

INGREDIENTS

2 cups steel cut oats

2 cups cauliflower rice

5 cups water

DIRECTIONS

Pressure cook on high for 4 minutes and use the natural release.

HOT FLASH TIP

1. Don't forget to top individual bowls with whatever fruit, nuts, seeds, yogurt or milk you want.

BUTTERMILK

If you don't have buttermilk hanging out in your fridge, and honestly why would you when it's so easy to make your own, here's an easy recipe.

INGREDIENTS

1 TB vinegar or freshly squeezed Lemon Juice*

1 cup milk

DIRECTIONS

Mix the ingredients together and let it stand a few minutes until thickened.

HOT FLASH TIPS

1. *The benefit to making your own buttermilk is that you can use dairy or a plant-based milk, and you can make as much or as little as you need.*

CARDAMOM & BANANA FILLING

A delicious and lovely twist on the traditional cinnamon and brown sugar filling.

INGREDIENTS

1/4 cup butter, softened
1 banana, mashed
1/4 cup unsweetened applesauce

1/4 cup brown sugar
1 1/2 tsp cinnamon
1 1/2 tsp cardamom

DIRECTIONS

Mix all ingredients together and use in Mamma G's Cinnamon Buns* recipe or whatever you'd like!

HOT FLASH TIP

1. *Store the leftovers in the fridge for up to 3 days.*
2. *This is also delicious spread over pancakes or waffles.*

CHUNKY CINNAMON APPLESAUCE

Oh my gosh, I love homemade applesauce! It's so much better than store bought. If I'm not making a crumble or pie, I like to make a big batch and freeze it in little containers. Apples are one of those foods that I've attached to wonderful childhood memories, so the smell of fresh apples or apples cooking with cinnamon takes me right back to Nova Scotia when we would go apple picking and my mother would make apple pie and Apple Crumble*.

INGREDIENTS

5 lb bag of McIntosh apples or any other soft, sweet apple

$1/4$ cup water

1 – 2 TB brown sugar

2 tsp cinnamon

$1/4$ tsp nutmeg

DIRECTIONS

1. Peel and slice the apples and put them into a large saucepan along with the water, brown sugar, cinnamon and nutmeg.
2. Bring to a boil, reduce heat to medium-low, cover and let the apples simmer for about 15 to 20 minutes until tender.
3. Remove the cover and cook for another 5 to 10 minutes until thickened.
4. Mash roughly with a potato masher and store in a container in the fridge.

HOT FLASH TIP

1. *If you have a crockpot, let this simmer on low for 6 to 8 hours and allow it to fill your home with the sweet aroma of fall.*
2. *This recipe uses the same ingredients as the apple mixture in my Apple Crumble*, but the cooking method is slightly different. If you have a lot of apples, use some to make an apple crumble and some for applesauce.*

CREAMY CHAMPAGNE DRESSING

I love to make my own salad dressings. It saves money and my sanity knowing the ingredients I use are the healthiest choice for us. This is one of our favorite dressings and goes especially well with arugula, kale or romaine lettuce.

INGREDIENTS

1/4 cup champagne vinegar

1 TB freshly squeezed Lemon Juice*

1/3 cup extra virgin olive oil

1 TB yellow mustard

2 TB maple syrup

1 garlic clove, minced

1/4 – 1/2 tsp salt

DIRECTIONS

Whisk all ingredients together and store it in a cute little mason jar in the fridge.

HOT FLASH TIP

1. *Make sure to let the dressing come to room temp before using because an excellent quality olive oil will solidify in the fridge.*

CREAMY JALAPEÑO SAUCE

This creamy jalapeño sauce is so delicious, you'd never guess it's dairy free. Made with simple ingredients, it's an easy way to sneak more veggies and beans into your healthy balanced diet. Serve over potatoes, roasted veggies, nachos, eggs benny, cooked noodles or use as the base for cream soups.

INGREDIENTS

4 cups Yukon Gold potatoes, peeled & diced

1/4 cup onion, diced

1/4 cup low sodium white beans, drained & rinsed

1/4 cup raw cashews

5 TB nutritional yeast

1 jalapeño pepper, seeded

2 tsp freshly squeezed Lemon Juice*

2 tsp garlic powder

1/2 tsp sea salt

1 cup starchy water, reserved from the potatoes

2 cups water

DIRECTIONS

1. Place the potatoes and onion in a large pot, cover with water and cook until tender. Reserve 1 C of the starchy water when you drain them.
2. In a powerful blender, place the potatoes, onions, beans, cashews, yeast, jalapeño pepper, lemon juice, garlic powder, salt, 1 C of the reserved starchy water and the 2 C of water.
3. Blend until smooth, adding more water if it's too thick (it will thicken even more as it sits).

HOT FLASH TIP

1. *Before pouring this into your containers, give it a taste and add more salt if needed. If you're not going to use it within a few days, pour it into two containers and freeze one. It does get watery once frozen, but reheated, it will be fine.*

CREAMY RANCH DRESSING

I love having homemade dressings lined up in the fridge in cute little mason jars. I find with homemade dressings, it's best to make them the day before so the flavors can cozy up to each other and the herbs have a chance to release all of their amazing flavors.

INGREDIENTS

- 1/2 cup plain Greek yogurt
- 1/2 cup mayonnaise
- 1/4 cup Buttermilk*
- 1 garlic clove, minced
- 1 TB chives, finely chopped
- 1/2 tsp dried dill weed
- 1/4 tsp sea salt
- 1/8 tsp ground pepper

DIRECTIONS

1. Whisk all the ingredients together and then taste it. Does it need a bit more of anything? Add it now and then store it in a container in the fridge.

HOT FLASH TIPS

1. Make this recipe even easier with my Ranch Dressing Dry Spice Mix*. You can make a little or a lot of dressing as needed.

DATE PASTE

Date paste is a natural sweetener loaded with vitamins, minerals and fiber. When the dates are blended with water, they take on a caramel-like consistency and can be used in many different recipes in place of sugar, honey or maple syrup.

INGREDIENTS

1 cup soft medjool dates

$1/2$ cup boiling water

DIRECTIONS

1. Let the dates sit in the boiling water for 10 minutes.
2. Put the dates and water into a small high-speed blender and blend until smooth.

HOT FLASH TIP

1. Keep leftovers in a covered container in the fridge for up to three months or freeze in smaller containers.
2. Use it as a dip for sliced fruit, to sweeten and thicken homemade dressings and sauces, spread on toast with a sprinkle of cinnamon, add to oatmeal, mix with a little balsamic vinegar or serve with grilled meats.
3. You can also substitute date paste in many recipes that call for sugar, honey, or maple syrup as a healthier alternative.

FRESH BASIL PESTO

One of my favorite sauces is a fresh tasting basil pesto, which can be used with pizza, pasta or spooned onto fresh sourdough toast. Sure, you could buy pesto, but it's so easy to make. And besides, the store-bought ones are overloaded with oil and sodium. (be still, my overbeating heart). You can make this with pine nuts, walnuts, raw cashews or raw almonds.

INGREDIENTS

2 cups fresh basil leaves

2 TB freshly squeezed Lemon Juice*

$1/2$ cup freshly grated Romano or Parmesan cheese (no dry imitation stuff)

$1/4$ cup pine nuts

2 garlic cloves, minced

$1/3$ cup extra virgin olive oil

salt & pepper to taste

DIRECTIONS

1. Pack the basil leaves into a food processor and give it a few pulses before adding the remaining ingredients.
2. Pulse until it's well mixed.
3. Taste it. Does it need a bit of salt and pepper? Add it now.
4. Keep it in a mason jar in the fridge and use within one week.

HOT FLASH TIP

1. When buying a good quality olive oil, the name of where the olives come from should be on the bottle and it should say "extra virgin olive oil," otherwise known as cold-pressed.
2. You can use a different type of nut in place of pine nuts if you prefer. Consider trying this recipe with almonds, cashews or walnuts.
3. Pesto is so versatile! Use it on your pizza, in your pastas, on your grilled cheese or your burgers.

GREEK TZATZIKI SAUCE

Once you see how easy and quick it is to make your own tzatziki, you'll never buy it from a store again. Even though this recipe is lower in fat and sodium than store bought, it's creamy, delicious and full of fresh, clean flavors. Serve it with grilled meats, as a condiment with falafels or as a dip with grilled veggies.

INGREDIENTS

1 medium English cucumber, finely grated & strained

1 cup plain 2% Greek yogurt

2 garlic cloves, minced

1 TB freshly squeezed Lemon Juice*

1 – 2 tsp dried dill weed

$\frac{1}{4}$ tsp onion powder

$\frac{1}{2}$ tsp salt

black pepper to taste

DIRECTIONS

1. Let the grated cucumber sit in a strainer for 5 to 10 minutes to get rid of as much water as possible. You can gently press down on it with a paper towel to help it along.
2. Combine the yogurt, garlic, lemon juice, dill, onion, salt and pepper.
3. Taste it. Does it need a bit more of anything? Add it now.
4. Fold in the grated cucumber and refrigerate.

HOT FLASH TIP

1. *You can make this recipe even easier by mixing the yogurt and cucumber with 1 T of my Lemon & Dill Dry Spice Mix*.*

HOLLANDAISE SAUCE

While writing this book, my editor told me she had a yummy recipe for hollandaise sauce. Of course, I asked if I could see it because I just had to try it. Well, my friend, with Mandi's permission, I knew I had to put it in this book because it's that good! This is a fast-paced recipe, but it really is simple to make and scrumptious to eat. Eggs benny would simply be eggs on muffins if not for the rich, buttery, and tangy hollandaise sauce that we all love and adore. Make this just prior to poaching your eggs so it's nice and warm when you serve it up.

INGREDIENTS

3 egg yolks
1 TB freshly squeezed Lemon Juice*
$1/8$ tsp salt

$1/8$ tsp pepper to taste
$1/2$ cup (1 cube) butter
2 TB boiling water

DIRECTIONS

1. In a bowl, whisk the egg yolks, lemon juice, salt and pepper together. Set this aside.
2. Melt the butter in a small pot until foamy, but do not burn it.
3. Turn the burner off to allow the pot to cool slightly while you whisk the butter into the yolk mixture. Continue to whisk the ingredients in the bowl for a few more seconds. You will feel it start to thicken already as the hot butter slightly cooks the yolks.
4. Pour it all back into the pot and stir constantly over low heat until slightly thickened. Be sure not to overcook it or you will end up with scrambled eggs instead of a sauce.
5. Turn the burner off and pour it all back into the bowl.
6. Whisk in the hot water and serve over eggs benedict.

HOT FLASH TIPS

1. Save the egg whites from this recipe to use in others that don't require the yolks, such as my Country Brunch Pancakes* or Chocolate Cake with Marshmallow Frosting*.
2. Low and slow is the way to go with a hollandaise sauce. You will need to stir constantly and be diligent about the cook time—you want a smooth sauce, not scrambled eggs. If you have an immersion blender, this is the time to use it. Practice mindfulness as you make this recipe.
3. Mandi recommends making your eggs benny with bacon instead of ham, or even taking it up another notch and using crab! You can also toss in some smoked salmon, sliced avocados, tomatoes or steamed spinach, and in place of English muffins, you could use biscuits, potato pancakes, regular pancakes, waffles, or focaccia bread.
4. Refrigerate any leftovers and use it with baked salmon, beef steaks, roasted veggies or as a dip for homemade French fries.

HOMEMADE PIZZA DOUGH

Homemade pizza crust is so much better than store bought, and whether you make it by hand, use a bread machine or a stand mixer, you can always make extra for the freezer. This recipe makes four 12-inch pizzas and it takes 2 hours to rise, so keep that in mind when you're making a batch.

INGREDIENTS

2 1/2 cups warm water

2 tsp sugar

2 tsp instant yeast

7 cups all-purpose flour

1 tsp salt

6 TB olive oil

DIRECTIONS

1. In a medium bowl, whisk the warm water, sugar and yeast together. Let it sit and bubble for 5 minutes.
2. Place the flour into a large bowl.
3. Whisk the salt and olive oil into the yeast mixture and pour it into the middle of the flour. Using your hands, knead until it's well mixed.
4. Dump the dough out onto a floured counter and knead for 10 to 15 minutes or until smooth and elastic. Shape it into a ball.
5. Put the dough back into the large bowl. Place a tiny bit of olive oil in your hands, rub them together and then rub them all over the dough.
6. Cover the bowl with a light tea towel and let it sit in a warm place for 2 hours to rise.
7. Punch the dough down to release any bubbles and start shaping it into rustic pizzas.

HOT FLASH TIPS

1. *Make it an herb crust by adding 1 tsp oregano, 1/2 tsp basil and 1 tsp garlic powder to the flour.*

2. Looking for a warm, draft-free place to let your dough rise? If you have an over-the-stove microwave, turn the light on and put your dough inside. It's the perfect temperature.

3. <u>To freeze:</u> Once the dough is finished rising, wrap it and store in a covered container in the freezer. When you're ready to use it, remove it from the freezer and let the dough sit out at room temperature (still covered) for about 4 to 6 hours.

4. Always prebake your crust for 5 minutes before putting any toppings on. This will prevent an undercooked soggy crust.

ICING SUGAR

If you don't keep icing sugar on hand, it's easy to make as much as you need with the regular granulated sugar found in most pantries.

INGREDIENTS

1 cup granulated sugar

1 TB cornstarch

DIRECTIONS

1. Place both ingredients in a high-speed blender and blend for about 30 seconds until it looks and feels like icing sugar.
2. Store in an airtight container.

HOT FLASH TIPS

1. *When a recipe calls for icing sugar, do not make the mistake of using regular granulated sugar. It will not turn out with the desired consistency, and it's so simple to turn it into the right product with this recipe.*

LEMON CURD

I love lemon curd, but making it always frustrated me because you had to separate the yolks from the whites, and I'm not the most patient person when it comes to that. One day, I decided to try making it with whole eggs instead, thinking what's the worst thing that could happen? Well, my friend, it turned out great! You can use this sweet tart deliciousness as a spread on scones, layer with yogurt and granola for a delicious parfait, add white balsamic vinegar and olive oil for a delicious salad dressing, spoon it into prebaked tart shells and top with my Marshmallow Frosting* or add it to frozen bananas and make a lovely lemon ice cream in your blender.

INGREDIENTS

1/2 cup freshly squeezed Lemon Juice*
2 tsp Lemon Zest*
1/2 cup sugar

3 large eggs
5 TB butter

DIRECTIONS

1. In a medium saucepan, whisk the lemon juice, zest, sugar and eggs together.
2. Cook over medium heat until it starts to get thick and begins to bubble.
3. Stir in the butter.
4. Remove from the heat and store in the fridge in a covered container.

HOT FLASH TIPS

1. *If you're not going to use the curd within a week, pour it into silicone muffin cups, freeze, pop them out and store them in a freezer-safe container.*
2. *Use this in my Sheet Pan Lemon Chicken & Rosemary Potatoes* recipe, or on nearly any breakfast recipe.*

LEMON & DILL DRY SPICE MIX

Who doesn't love spices! I admit I have a mild obsession with spices but don't have the room to store them all. If you have a small kitchen or are limited in space, do what I do. Combine them! My sister-in-law Melinda does this with condiments. Instead of throwing away almost empty jars, she mixes all the little bits together and creates one brand-new condiment. Brilliant!

INGREDIENTS

4 tsp dill weed

2 tsp garlic powder

2 tsp dried Lemon Zest*

1 tsp onion flakes

$1/4$ tsp salt

DIRECTIONS

1. Blend all the ingredients together and store it in a glass jar.

HOT FLASH TIPS

1. Make a dip with this recipe by mixing 1 T of the dry spice mix with 1 C mayo, sour cream or yogurt.
2. This dry spice mix can also be used to make my Greek Tzatziki Sauce* even easier.
3. Add this dry spice mix to my Open-Faced Tuna Salad Cheese Buns* recipe.

LEMON ZEST & LEMON JUICE

I know not everyone has dried lemon zest on hand, but if you're thrifty like me, you can make your own easily. Buy a bag of lemons (they're cheaper in bulk), zest and then squeeze the juice from each one. Easy peasy lemon squeezy, you've got yourself a double whammy!

INGREDIENTS

lemons, lemons & more lemons (that's it!)

DIRECTIONS

<u>Lemon Zest</u>

1. Use a hand grater to zest the lemons. Lay the zest out on a large pan and freeze. Once frozen, keep half in a little freezer-safe container for making lemon loaves, muffins, soups and chowders. Dry out the other half and use it for seasonings.

<u>Lemon Juice</u>

1. Squeeze the juice from the lemons and either keep it in a jar in the fridge to be used up within one week or pour it into an ice cube tray. Typically, each cube holds about 1 T. Once frozen, transfer to a freezer-safe container and use them whenever a recipe calls for fresh lemon juice.

HOT FLASH TIPS

1. Make sure you zest before juicing! Use the fine part of your grater to zest the lemon. When you're ready to juice them, if your lemons seem hard, roll them around on the counter with your hands or pop them into the microwave for 20 seconds. That should help release the juice and make your job easier.
2. It's more economical to buy a large bag of lemons and make both lemon zest and lemon juice at the same time to keep both ingredients on hand.
3. Generally speaking, a large lemon is equal to about 3 T of juice, while a medium lemon is equal to 2 T of juice. Depending on how fresh your lemons are, 2 to 3 lemons should yield $1/2$ C of juice.

OAT FLOUR

Call me crazy, but why would you buy a bag of oat flour when it's so much easier and cheaper to make it yourself? You do need a powerful blender, so I'll forgive you if you don't have one of those, but it will pay for itself if you use oat flour a lot.

INGREDIENTS

dry oats

DIRECTIONS

1. Put the oats into a blender and blend at a high speed for about 1 minute until it resembles flour. Seriously could it be any easier!

HOT FLASH TIP

1. *Make a large batch and store it in your pantry for easy use.*

PICKLED RED ONIONS

Such an easy, pretty little condiment that tastes amazing on sandwiches, burgers, salads, poke bowls and even omelets.

INGREDIENTS

1 red onion, peeled & thinly sliced

$3/4$ cup boiling water

$3/4$ cup apple cider vinegar

$1/4$ cup honey

$1/2$ tsp salt

$1/2 - 1/4$ tsp red pepper flakes

DIRECTIONS

1. Put the sliced onions into a clean mason jar.
2. Combine the boiling water, vinegar, honey, salt and red pepper flakes.
3. Pour the hot liquid over the onions, put the lid on, give it a shaky shake and let them sit on the counter until cooled down enough to refrigerate.
4. These should last about two weeks in the fridge.

HOT FLASH TIP

1. *You can substitute $1/4$ C sugar or maple syrup if you don't have any honey in the pantry.*

PLUMP RAISINS

If you put shriveled up raisins in your baking recipes, they're going to stay that way and I know you don't want that.

INGREDIENTS

raisins

boiling water

DIRECTIONS

1. Cover the raisins in a bowl with boiling water. Let them soak for a few minutes and drain before using.

HOT FLASH TIPS

1. *Love the flavor of rum-soaked raisins but don't want the alcohol? Add a few drops of rum extract to the boiling water.*

POULTRY SEASONING

Use this in your favorite stuffing recipe, gravy, soups, on chicken, turkey, game hens or any poultry you want.

INGREDIENTS

$1/2$ tsp dried sage
$1/2$ tsp thyme

DIRECTIONS

1. Mix the two herbs together. That's it!

HOT FLASH TIPS

1. *Use this in my Chicken Stew with Fluffy Dumplings* recipe!*

PUMPKIN PIE SPICE SEASONING

Who doesn't love autumn? Snuggly blankets, hot cups of tea or cocoa, and pumpkin pie—how can you go wrong? This seasoning mix is crazy easy to make for all your fall dessert recipes.

INGREDIENTS

1 tsp cinnamon

1/4 tsp allspice

DIRECTIONS

1. Mix the two spices together and you're done!

HOT FLASH TIPS

1. *This goes beautifully in my Pumpkin Glory Muffins*, but you can use it in a plethora of fall dessert recipes!*

RANCH DRESSING DRY SPICE MIX

Having your own ranch dressing mix on hand means no more expired bottles of dressing lurking in the back of your fridge. We actually prefer this recipe to any store-bought brand because it's really versatile. Use it for a dip or dressing, add it to flour when coating chicken or fish and sprinkle it over roasted veggies.

INGREDIENTS

- 1/2 cup buttermilk powder
- 1 tsp garlic powder
- 1 tsp onion powder
- 1 tsp dried chives
- 1 TB dried parsley
- 1/2 tsp smoked paprika
- 1/4 tsp salt
- 1/4 tsp freshly ground pepper

DIRECTIONS

1. Mix all the spices together and store until you are ready to use it.

HOT FLASH TIPS

1. Make this into a dressing by whisking 1 T of the dry spice mix with 1/4 C mayo and 1/4 C plain Greek yogurt. Slowly add milk until you get the consistency you want (about 2 T).
2. To make a dip, whisk 2 T of the dry spice mix with 1/4 C mayo and 1/4 C plain Greek yogurt (do not add milk because you want your dip to be thicker than the dressing).

ROASTED BROCCOLI

I find steamed broccoli kind of boring, unless smothered in warm hollandaise sauce, but once you roast it, Oh My Gosh! It's like eating an entirely new vegetable.

INGREDIENTS

1 head of broccoli, trimmed & separated into florets

1 TB olive or avocado oil

2 TB freshly squeezed Lemon Juice*

2 TB honey

$1/2$ tsp sea salt

2 cloves garlic, thinly sliced

DIRECTIONS

1. In a large bowl with a lid, gently toss the broccoli florets with the oil, lemon juice, honey, salt and garlic. Or just get your hands in there because that's pretty satisfying.
2. Preheat your air fryer to 400°F and set the timer for 8 minutes.
3. Once it's preheated, add your broccoli to the basket.
4. When your machine tells you to flip your food, just get in there and give the broccoli a little toss.

HOT FLASH TIP

1. *Don't have an air fryer? Roast the broccoli in the oven instead. Toss the broccoli with the same ingredients. Put everything on a parchment-lined baking sheet and roast at 400°F for about 25 minutes or until they start to brown.*

SAUSAGE PATTIES

Making your own sausage patties is hands-down my favorite way to eat sausages. These are big on flavor with a hint of sweetness from the green apple.

INGREDIENTS

2 lb ground pork

2 green apples, grated (you can either leave the peel on or remove it)

2 TB green onions, finely chopped

2 tsp fennel

2 tsp sage

1 tsp sea salt

1/2 tsp white pepper

DIRECTIONS

1. In a large bowl, combine the pork, apple, onions, fennel, sage, salt and pepper. Shape into 12 thin patties. Fry them in a little oil over medium heat until browned on both sides and cooked through.

HOT FLASH TIPS

1. *These freeze really well and are quick to reheat in the microwave, although I prefer to wrap them in foil and pop them in the toaster oven.*

STABILIZED WHIPPED CREAM

Forgot to buy whipped cream for your pumpkin pie or hot cocoa? No problem! Making your own is as easy as one, two, three!

INGREDIENTS

1 cup heavy whipping cream
1 TB Icing Sugar*
1 tsp vanilla extract
1 TB instant vanilla pudding mix, or $\frac{1}{4}$ tsp cream of tartar

DIRECTIONS

1. Using a stand mixer or hand blender, whip the cream until soft peaks form. Add the icing sugar, vanilla and either the pudding or cream of tartar, and carry-on whipping until the peaks are firmer.

HOT FLASH TIPS

1. *You can substitute powdered sugar for the icing sugar or make your own Icing Sugar* with my simple recipe.*

SWEET RUM SAUCE

I use this mostly with my Sourdough Bread Pudding* recipe, but this pairs wonderfully with other things as well.

INGREDIENTS

14 oz can sweetened condensed milk
2 TB butter
1 tsp water
1 tsp cornstarch
1 – 2 tsp rum extract

DIRECTIONS

1. Heat the condensed milk and butter in a saucepan over medium heat until the butter is melted and the mixture is hot.
2. In a bowl, whisk the water, cornstarch and extract together and stir into the milk mixture.
3. Continue to stir until it comes to a boil, and then remove it from the heat.

HOT FLASH TIPS

1. Drizzle over fruit salad, baked yams, French toast, pancakes or waffles.

TOASTED NUTS

Toasting your nuts prior to adding them to any recipe will bring a more intense flavor into the mix.

INGREDIENTS

whatever kind of nuts you want to use

DIRECTIONS

1. Preheat the oven to 325°F.
2. Spread the nuts out onto a parchment-lined baking sheet and bake for about 10 minutes or until they start to brown and smell fragrant.
3. Let them cool down completely before storing.

HOT FLASH TIP

1. *It's more economical to buy a large bag and toast them as soon as you get home. We like to put half into airtight containers in the pantry (these will get used up quickly), and the other half into the freezer. You can either use the original bag or a freezer-safe container.*

Conclusion

Well, my friend, our time together has come to an end—at least, for now. Within the pages of this book, I have bared my way of life to you. Having discovered a way to create and maintain balance in my own life, my hope is that by using the methods and recipes in this book, you can too. In fact, I know you can, and it doesn't mean you have to go on some crazy diet or completely give up your favorite foods. Balance simply means a little of this and a little of that. So, remember to take the "good" with the "bad" (but don't forget, those are curse words in my cookbook).

As Meno-Positive Chicks, we may have enjoyed a few birthdays to our names, but listen up ladies: taking a line from Monty Python's Holy Grail… "I'm not dead yet." While we're still breathing, we need to be actively working on our health and creating balance. Just like a chair, we need to maintain the strength and integrity of each leg so the chair can support us. To keep our bodies as healthy as they can be, we need to strive for a healthy relationship with our food, get plenty of rest, find the calm within, move our bodies, and build our community.

Creating balance is a practice that takes time and commitment, but it's well worth it. Notice how I have purposefully used the word "create" rather than "find" in relation to balance throughout this book. This is because we are in control! At the end of the day, we are the only ones who can create more balance within our lives. If you remember nothing else, my friend, my hope is that you remember that we are all human and life is a constant work in progress, but if you actively partake in creating balance in your life, you are making progress (cheers to that, my friend!).

I would love to support you on your journey to create balance in your own life. Let's join together and build a tribe of powerful and confident women who are committed to creating and maintaining balance in our lives. Visit the Meno-Positive Chicks website often and subscribe to our newsletter—we have a few more irons in the fire that I just know you're going to enjoy. Trust me, you don't want to miss out.

And finally, if you enjoyed this book, one of the greatest compliments you could give me is to leave an honest review on Amazon.

With much love, a little cheese and a whole lot of warm fuzzies,

Darlene

www.meno-positive-chicks.com

Acknowledgments

It took a village to bring this book to fruition and I will forever be grateful to those of you who were part of this journey.

My family: Big Bear, Ben, Rebecca & Rob, thank you for believing in me even if you secretly thought I'd never get this book finished. Special thanks to Rob for the cover idea!

My friends: Michelle and Tasha, thank you for always being there for me whenever I had doubts or questions.

My friend, Jennifer: Without you, I might not have ever written this book. Our paths crossed many years ago and we had no idea where it was going to lead. I now have a career I love and I owe a lot of that to you. Bet you didn't see that coming, did ya?

To my editor, Mandi Summit, and the incredible support team at Self-Publishing School: You all believed in me and my project. Your guidance kept me on track throughout this entire process and kept my nerves at bay, knowing I was in good hands.

And finally, YOU, my friend: I'd like to thank you for reading this book. Your support means the world to me, and I sincerely hope you will join our tribe of Meno-Positive Chicks!

About Me, the Author

Hello friend,

As I sit here wondering what to tell you about who I am, the thing that keeps popping into my head is that I'm probably a lot like you in many ways. I have a background in nutrition, fitness, real estate and finance, but I also love coffee and have way more mugs than I care to admit. I enjoy reading and can often be found snuggled up in a comfy chair with a cozy blanket reading books about healthy living, historical fiction and, of course, recipe books.

I'm a wife to a very patient, kind, hard-working man. We live in a lovely home close to the ocean where we can hear the whales and sea lions play and feel the fresh ocean breeze through our windows. This year, we celebrated our 34th wedding anniversary with many more to come. We have two amazing adult kids and one future son-in-law. I know it sounds cliche, but they really are my world, and maybe one day I'll be blessed with grandchildren too.

Nothing fills my heart more than spending time with family and friends, especially sharing a meal. I view the act of gathering around the kitchen table as a safe place where relationships are nourished and supported. Because of this, my kitchen has always been the heart of our home throughout the years. Food was never just about fueling our body; it's one of the ways I was able to show my love to my family and friends, and now I can share it with you through this recipe book.

I truly believe that balance starts at home. So, my friend, get on your apron, play some music to set the mood, and move your body as you create a lovely home-cooked meal.

Manufactured by Amazon.ca
Bolton, ON

33154414R00081